M000211474

LET'S TALK

ROBERT L. RANDALL

LET'S
TALK

helping couples, groups,
and individuals
communicate

United Church Press | Cleveland, Ohio

United Church Press, Cleveland, Ohio 44115
© 1997 by Robert L. Randall

Biblical quotations are from the New Revised Standard Version of the Bible,
© 1989 by the Division of Christian Education of the National Council of the
Churches of Christ in the U.S.A., and are used by permission

All rights reserved. Published 1997

Printed in the United States of America on acid-free paper

02 01 00 99 98 97   5 4 3 2 1

Library of Congress Cataloging-in-Publication Data
Randall, Robert L., 1942–   •
     Let's talk : helping couples, groups, and individuals communicate
  / Robert L. Randall
        p.   cm.
     Includes bibliographical references.
     ISBN 0-8298-1214-8 (pbk. : alk. paper)
     1. Interpersonal communication—Religious aspects—Christianity.
  2. Pastoral counseling.   I. Title.
  BV4319.R26   1997
  253'.5—dc21   97-25732
                                                              CIP

CONTENTS

LISTENING TO PARISHIONERS

P astor, my husband and I need to see you. We aren't communicating well at all."

"Something has to be done with the committee, Reverend. We're not getting through to each other." "Could you come over to the house? She needs someone she can talk to."

Within an ordinary week, pastors hear many comments like these from parishioners. Our first reaction is to wonder why the couple is not getting along, why the committee is stuck, or what the individual needs to talk about.

If we listen carefully to these comments, however, we will hear parishioners already telling us what they understand the difficulties to be: problems in communication. In a variety of ways, parishioners diagnose their troubles as problems in communicating. Their requests for help with communication are among the most frequent concerns brought to us clergy.

Why should that be? Because parishioners implicitly know that the quality of human communication and the quality of human relationships go hand in hand. They experience how breakdowns in communication result in broken ties. They yearn for help from pastoral caregivers to heal their communication problems and reconnect them to others.

Although pastors are asked to solve communication problems, rarely do we address these problems directly. This occurs for two reasons. First, we tend to consider communication problems as secondary rather than primary, as symptoms rather than causes. Our training in pastoral care and counseling is typically based on some form of depth psychology. We are taught to listen for the covert message beneath the overt message and to take the presenting problem as symptomatic of more basic difficulties.

Consequently, we have a tendency to minimize a parishioner's definition of a problem as one of communication.

I have been guilty of this error for years. As a pastoral counselor trained in psychoanalysis, I habitually listened for the dynamics beneath the content—which means I did not pay much attention to how individuals defined their problems. But they kept coming back with a persistent interpretation of their difficulties, not one about sex or money but about communication: "If only we could learn to talk together again, things would be all right." My education began anew when they finally got through to me that I was not hearing what they were saying.

Second, we clergy tend to consider communication work as prefatory rather than major. For example, we might help a couple open lines of communication as an initial step in dealing with their problems, but we rarely use a communication approach as a major intervention. Aiding communication, consequently, once again becomes secondary rather than primary.

This book takes seriously the yearnings of parishioners for help with their communication problems. It affirms the respect we pastoral caregivers must give to the wisdom and requests of those seeking our help. The book also affirms that problematic communication itself leads to relational difficulties, rather than just the reverse. How people communicate shapes how they think and feel about themselves and how they relate to others. We can make an adjustment in our pastoral understanding and intervention with parishioners when we acknowledge the primary influence of problematic communication.

In this book I present various pastoral approaches to communication problems. These approaches can be helpful not only in pastoral counseling but in all pastoral care activities with parishioners, for the essence of ministry is communication. For the sake of explanation, however, we will focus on communication counseling with couples, church groups, and individuals.

Chapter 1 outlines a particular interpretation of communication developed from my twenty-five years' experience as a pastoral counselor and clinical psychologist in a church setting. (Besides providing psychotherapy for pastors and their families, I provide consultation to clergy, congregations, and denominational bodies.)

People can be understood to operate from four basic forms of communication. These forms are depicted in the following diagram.

FORMS OF COMMUNICATION
EVALUATIVE
INTERPRETATIVE
FEELING
PRAGMATIC

People employing the *pragmatic* form of communication are focused on problem solving. People speaking from the *feeling* form of communication are expressing subjective experiences. Those using the *interpretative* form of communication are giving explanations. Those speaking from the *evaluative* form of communication are making value judgments.

Understanding how people use these communication forms can enhance caregiving efforts of pastors and also provide a tool for assessing particular communication difficulties. Relationships suffer, for example, when people do not communicate in the same form or when one communication form dominates the others. Even when communication problems are clearly secondary, that is, symptomatic of underlying relational struggles, this model of communication can orient one's caregiving efforts.

Chapter 2 discusses how specific communication problems cause stress for couples and tells how clergy can counsel them. Chapter 3 describes how communication problems interfere with the work of groups in the church and discusses how we can guide them. Chapters 4 and 5 highlight communication problems of distressed individuals and suggest how we can aid them informed by this communication theory. The broader goal, as I have said, is to depict approaches to communication problems that can be used with persons in a variety of settings.

The approaches I describe can be put into practice by any reasonably competent minister. Training in psychology is not required. In other words, you do not have to be a certified pastoral counselor in order to understand these approaches and use them.

The basic premise throughout the book is this: People are constantly formed and restored by the communication that passes between them. The very word *communicate* comes from a Latin word meaning "to participate." Helping parishioners communicate with each other is helping them participate with one another. Pastoral care of communication problems, therefore, is a ministry of high calling.

Understanding communication problems begins with understanding the communication forms people use. From my counseling work I have discerned four basic patterns: pragmatic, feeling, interpretative, and evaluative. People in therapy communicate in problem-solving ways, in emotive ways, in explaining ways, and/or in assessing ways. One couple dealing with divorce communicated systematically about litigation and what to tell the children (pragmatic communication). At certain points they found themselves communicating expressively about their fears and broken dreams (feeling communication). At other times they communicated reflectively about how they had arrived at this predicament and what it meant for their future (interpretative communication). Not infrequently they communicated judgmentally about each other's strengths and faults (evaluative communication).

These communication forms are not confined just to counseling. I have observed, for instance, that people communicate to bereaved individuals in the same four modes. Parishioners attending wakes may relate primarily in a problem-centered manner: "If there is anything I can do for you, don't hesitate to call me." "Come and sit down. You've been standing by the casket for hours." "I'll arrange a luncheon at the church after the funeral. Don't worry about it." This is pragmatic communication.

Parishioners may approach bereaved individuals on an emotional level: "I broke down when I heard he died." "I know what you're going through." "I just wanted to run right over and throw my arms around you." "My heart goes out to you and your family. Please accept my sympathies." This is feeling communication.

People may relate to grieving parishioners by offering explanations (interpretative communication): "She would have wanted to die this way." "This is a hard time, but God will stand by to strengthen you."

1

"We all have to go through the stages of grieving." "There is meaning in all this suffering. It just isn't clear right now."

Finally, parishioners may use evaluative communication to express their assessments to the bereaved: "He certainly was a wonderful person." "You were a good spouse to the very end." "She got what she deserved." "You'll be better off without him."

My work with groups indicates that they also communicate in these basic forms. Staff meetings with my colleagues entail a mixture of all four. We work on decisions that have to be made (pragmatic communication). We share how life is for us personally (feeling communication). We try to make sense of behavior and to find meaning in what happens in the congregation's life (interpretative communication). We extend praise for work well done, but sometimes find ourselves demeaning the efforts of others or making snide remarks (evaluative communication).

Churches in stress tend to revert to a single form of communication. They may become fixated in expression of emotions, for example. One church that deemed itself a dying congregation constantly spoke in grieving terms (feeling communication). Congregations likewise may wallow in self-recriminations or finger pointing (what we will later define as "critical evaluative communication"). Then again, they may be stuck in a constant analysis of their problem (interpretative communication).

Delineating the basic forms of communication as pragmatic, feeling, interpretative, and evaluative is not the only way to define types of communication. It does, however, have parallels with what we clergy commonly do in our work and with other typologies in psychology. For example, if an unmarried couple comes to us with an unexpected pregnancy, we are likely to do the following:

1. Talk about the realities that need to be faced (pragmatic communication).
2. Express empathy for the couple's reactions (feeling communication).

3. Explore what this event means to them and how they will integrate it into the rest of their life story (interpretative communication).

4. Discuss the moral issues surrounding this particular situation (evaluative communication).

Other studies support this notion of four basic forms of communication as described above. For example, William James designates four levels of psychological functioning: the practical level (parallel to pragmatic); the perceptual level (feeling); the conceptual level (interpretative); and the aesthetic and moral levels (evaluative).[1] The suggestion, furthermore, is that these four levels are specific "forms" of communication.

PRAGMATIC COMMUNICATION

M. Scott Peck begins his book *The Road Less Traveled* with the assessment that "life is a series of problems."[2] Life is difficult because the process of trying to solve problems is a painful one. Nonetheless, he asserts, this process of meeting and solving problems is also what gives life its meaning.

Implicit in what Peck says is the recognition that humankind possesses the capacity for problem solving. And indeed we do. One key form of our meaningful communication with each other is pragmatic communication, which is directed toward solving specific problems or generating an approach to problems. When using this form of communication, individuals look at the problem as realistically as possible. They gather data appropriate to the situation. They formulate solutions and test them, either through trying them out or conceptualizing their consequences. They acknowledge their limitations and rely upon suggestions from others.

Feeling, interpretative, and evaluative communication also occur in problem-solving situations to enhance pragmatic communication, but they do not dominate. For example, a membership committee was faced with the church's declining enrollment. "Our task," posed the chairperson, "is to come up with ways to increase our membership" (pragmatic communication). "I feel upset about what is happening to us," expressed one member (feeling communication), "and I think others do too" (interpretative communication). "Maybe that is one reason people don't join," responded a third person. "They may sense something of our anxiety and back off" (interpretative communication). "Then perhaps what we have to do first is to change our own way of thinking and feeling about the church," suggested another member. "Maybe we need to genuinely express joy about the life we already have here as a small congregation" (pragmatic communication). This committee as a group stayed basically in a pragmatic state of communication. The members did not dwell on feelings or interpretations. Instead, feeling and interpretative communications were used for the overarching purpose of communicating pragmatically.

Any issue can be communicated pragmatically. Married couples who are enraged with each other may communicate in an evaluative form filled with name calling and below-the-belt jabs (critical evaluative communication). Pastors counseling such couples can direct them to communicate pragmatically about how they can best handle situations at home when their relationship deteriorates to this condition.

One partner in the counseling, however, might say sarcastically, "No matter what we agree to, she won't do it when the time comes." The pastor may then say, "Then talk together about what you are going to do when one partner doesn't follow through with the agreement."

"I don't even want to talk to him *now*," the other partner may spit back, to which the pastor may say, "Then talk about what you're going to do in our counseling sessions when one of you refuses to talk to the other." The pastor keeps presenting the possibility and necessity of communicating pragmatically about situations where communication has become punishment.

Any expression, conversely, can represent pragmatic communication. For example, during a heated discussion a spouse may say to the angry partner, "Maybe we should take a break. This is really getting to you." These words may not be attempts to convey what the spouse is emotionally experiencing at the moment (they are not feeling communication). They may not be intended to illuminate the partner (they are not interpretative communication), nor to put the partner down (they are not evaluative communication). Instead, these words may be the spouse's pragmatic communication, a problem-solving effort to ease the tension lest the partner become injured or matters become worse.

A common tendency of people engaged in pragmatic communication is to take solving of problems as all-sufficient. One husband said to his wife, "Let's just make a list of what each of us needs to change to make our relationship better and that should take care of it." He was unaware that his habitual turn toward pragmatic communication contributed to the very problem he was trying to solve. Pragmatic communication is not a panacea. The minimal requirement for any relationship, however, is the ability of the participants to communicate pragmatically. People cannot get along, a more complex form of relating, if they are unable to make arrangements, a more elemental form of relating.

Pragmatic communication, however, influences relationships beyond the establishment of a workable environment. *Pragmatic communication can generate hope.* When a conflicted couple, for example, begins to talk about how to handle problems, even if they are not resolved, hope has a way of coming alive again. The couple begins to believe that life can be better between them and that they have the capacity to solve difficulties rather than suffer them. "Even if we don't always see eye to eye," said one spouse to the other, "we'll be fine if we just keep talking together about how to deal with things."

Similarly, *pragmatic communication can generate unity.* When a church group, for instance, experiences the satisfaction of having reached a decision, a sense of collegiality is established. Even when divisions exist within a group, the common effort of trying to resolve a problem can be a means by which people feel one in the Spirit. Social research has consistently shown that when people band together around the solving of a common problem, their differences recede and a sense of community begins to develop.

Finally, *pragmatic communication can generate wholeness.* For example, when a distressed individual makes an effort to talk about practical solutions, he or she may begin to feel healthier almost at once. Individuals not only communicate about solving their problems when they begin to feel well, they also begin to feel well when they communicate about solving their problems. Pragmatic communication is therapeutic. It generates momentum where one decision put in front of another propels the heart to take its own brave step. Even if tentative or play-acted, pragmatic communication has a way of moving people to take charge of their lives.

When pragmatic communication is lacking, however, no realistic hope can exist, unity wanes, and a sense of competence is diminished. When clergy care for parishioners' pragmatic communication, therefore, they touch the core of their lives. Pragmatic communication is, indeed, a means for giving and finding meaning in life.

FEELING COMMUNICATION

James B. Nelson in *Embodiment: An Approach to Sexuality and Christian Theology* reminds us that we engage the world through our bodily feelings. An affective dimension is always a part of the difficulties we encounter, for within our body we "feel" the problem. We also have feelings about events and relationships, about our past and our future, about where we are and who we are. Our feeling life goes on all the time, like our heartbeat. In a variety of ways we rely on this felt, bodily sense of things. Nelson quotes with approval W. B. Yeats's claim: "We only believe those thoughts which have been conceived not in the brain but in the whole body."[3]

Another key form of meaningful communication is feeling communication, the expression of what we experience in the whole body. Feeling communication includes reactions to specific events ("I was utterly blown away when the group acted without me"), expressions of emotion without a concrete subject ("I'm just feeling sad today"), as well as articulations of vague sensations "too deep for words" (Rom. 8:26).

Feeling communication seems to be our human effort/need to express our bodily felt sense of how life is for us. Through feeling communication we try to convey how we are experiencing our lived world at the moment. When a man speaks of feeling frightened, he is not simply talking about his emotions. He is telling about the current felt state of his existence. When a woman says she feels playful, she is not describing her sensations. She is conveying her felt sense about how she is engaging life, and how life is engaging her, at the moment. When a couple says, "Neither one of us feels loved by the other any more," they are not simply conveying hurt. They are conveying a painfully altered state of being. No matter what the content, each feeling communication expresses something of our felt sense of how we are in the world at the time.

Just as any issue can be approached with pragmatic communication, so can any situation can be approached with feeling communication. For example, a church council dealing with questions of what kind of furnace to buy or what type of toilet paper to order can appropriately talk about how they feel about these purchases, and how they feel these purchases will affect the feelings of parishioners. Each decision in the church is attached to the heart of a person whose sense of life's fairness and love's presence is affected in some way. Council members can, and should, engage in feeling communication when making decisions that impact on the lives of parishioners.

Even a lack of feeling can be approached by way of feeling communication. "I've just lost my job. I should feel something, but I don't," said one individual who was blocking his feelings. His minister then replied: "How does it feel not to have feelings?" This was an encouragement of the man's feelings as well as an assurance that he still had feelings. If the man had been so numb that he could not even talk about the feeling of having no feeling, then the minister might have functioned as an alter ego by expressing feelings for the man. "You might be feeling hollow inside right now, empty. It may even feel better being this way than feeling all knotted up with fear and anger."

Interpretations, evaluations, and pragmatic realities are typically involved but not dominant when individuals, couples, or groups engage in feeling communication. For example, when ministers call on hospitalized parishioners with the intention of giving them the opportunity to talk about their feelings, discussions about operating procedures (pragmatic communication), the future (interpretative communication), or the quality of care (evaluative communication) serve to stimulate emotional release (feeling communication).

Most often people engage in feeling communication simply to be understood. They just want others to "listen to my feelings" and "know what's inside me." When a woman confides to her pastor that she is burned out from taking care of her mother (who is stricken with Alzheimer's disease) and sometimes wishes her mother would die, she may not be looking for guidance (pragmatic communication), clarity (interpretative communication), or absolution (evaluative communication). She may simply want her pastor to understand how she feels.

People engaged in feeling communication are inclined to consider feelings as right or wrong, good or bad, and to make feelings the basis of decisions. Feelings in themselves are neither right nor wrong, good nor bad. They simply express a person's particular bodily felt sense of being in the world at a particular time. A bad feeling, strictly speaking, is either one construed as an ominous sign (interpretative communication), judged as a reprehensible reaction (evaluative communication), or approached as a pain to be relieved (pragmatic communication). A feeling in itself, however, is not bad, any more than a dream in and of itself, for example, is bad.

While our feelings do ground our thoughts, they alone cannot adequately determine our conduct. One minister did not dispute a man's expressed affection for a woman he had recently met, but he cautioned the man not to let those feelings solely determine his decision to leave his wife. In spite of the Human Potential Movement's admonition to "trust your gut," matters of the heart and matters of the head must constantly inform each other. In addition to consulted emotions (feeling communication), decisions require understanding (interpretative communication), clarification of values (evaluative communication), and anticipation of consequences (pragmatic communication).

Feeling communication is nonetheless necessary to human experience. On the one hand, *feeling communication grounds our individuality.* Our sense of reality is assured when we are in touch with our feelings. Our thoughts seem right when they resonate with our felt sense of things. We have an assured sense of who we are and where we are when we are able to articulate our feelings. Individuals who are out of touch with their feelings are out of touch with reality, with reason, and with their own identity.

Similarly, *feeling communication grounds our relationships.* We feel safely like others when experiences are validated as normal. Intimacies are formed and belonging is deepened when feelings are shared. The help of others is elicited through the expression of our feelings.

When feelings are suppressed, however, relationships suffer. We fantasize about being different. Acceptance into groups is made difficult. Empathy from others is not aroused. Pastors who care for the feeling communications of parishioners touch the very nature of their embodied existence.

INTERPRETATIVE COMMUNICATION

"The life of the self, be that the self of the person seeking help or of the pastoral helper, [can] be seen as fundamentally a process of interpretation."[4] Charles V. Gerkin bases his book *The Living Human Document: Re-Visioning Pastoral Counseling in a Hermeneutical Mode* on this premise—that from early in life people are presented with the necessity of interpreting what they experience. He explains how "the self as hermeneut [interpreter] and myth maker" is central in finding and living a meaningful life.

Gerkin points to another basic form of communication, interpretative communication, which is our attempt to explain our lived world. We try to define our feelings. We struggle to make sense of others' behavior and our own. We offer reasons for why something happened. We attempt to clarify meaning in something mysterious. Our interpretations open up our life by embracing answers as well as fashioning answers.

Our attempts at interpretative communication range from intuitive hunches to stories we generate about ourselves to scientific and theological proposals. Some feelings quickly crystallize in our mind and lead to spontaneous interpretations. Other interpretations unfold gradually as we constantly revise stories about who we were, who we are, and who we can become. Still other interpretations of our complex human existence require sustained conscious analysis. Whatever its nature, interpretative communication is our natural inclination to give structure and meaning to our experience.

Interpretative communication also shapes what we expect. What we anticipate, and thus how we respond, is determined by the interpretations we make about life. Meister Eckhart, the great German mystic, once said, "Become aware of what is in you. Announce it, pronounce it, produce it, and give birth to it." Perhaps he should have added: "But be careful how you name what is in you. It becomes that way." In large measure we live in response to the interpretations we give to our life. Events and issues themselves often do not cause us distress, but the interpretations we have made about them do.

As with pragmatic and feeling communication, interpretative communication can be applied to any situation. When Joseph confronted his betraying brothers in Egypt he spoke to them from an interpretative stance: "As for you, you meant evil against me; but God meant it for good, to bring it about that many people should be kept alive" (Gen. 50:20, RSV). Church members whose teenage son was stabbed to death by a home intruder supported themselves by speaking interpretatively:

"We keep reminding each other that God works in all things for good. Jim was a blessing to many of us in life. God will make him a blessing to us in death."

Interpretative communication likewise involves pragmatic, feeling, and evaluative communications to some degree. When a wife, for example, attempts to find a reason for her husband's infidelity, her interpretative efforts are informed by her feelings, by pragmatic considerations, and by her evaluation of him, herself, and the institution of marriage. Her effort to understand, her interpretative efforts, however, can remain primary.

A common tendency of people engaged in interpretative communication is to act as if their interpretations were facts. The old joke, "My mind is made up. Don't confuse me with the facts," could be amended to say, "My mind is made up. With that I have the facts." Groups in the church are prone to this tendency. Their interpretative communications may take on the aura of truth for them. Interpretations may move from being tentative explorations to becoming objective actualities. The more groups insulate themselves from outside interpretations that remind them of the limited, finite nature of their interpretations, the more inclined they are to construe their interpretations as factual realities.

Interpretative communication, however, is crucial for self-integration. *Life achieves order through our interpretations.* When Adam and Eve named creation, they participated with God in establishing an orderly existence. Interpretative communication creates structure from chaos. It provides a sense of constancy, predictability, and reliability necessary for productive work and internal security. Ultimate despair arises when life seems meaningless, or more accurately put, when an individual or group loses the capacity for meaningful interpretative communication. The capacity to generate an interpretation, no matter how outlandish, is a sign of remnant strength in an otherwise fragmented self.

Interpreting and reinterpreting our life helps us maintain vitality. Through our interpretative communication we not only structure our existence but also revise it. To remain vital, we must constantly rename ourselves. Self-integration is enhanced, for example, when we are able to reinterpret ourselves as aging moves us from one state to another. Self-esteem is increased when we are able to reinterpret ourselves in liberating ways. Our lives are redeemed, in parts and in large chunks, by the God-given capacity to reinterpret.

Interpretative communication helps us relate our situations to the total life process. Through interpretation we connect the relationships and events of our life to deeper issues of the soul. Interpretative communication makes it possible to have a life story and to integrate that story into ultimate realms of meaning. A pastor once said that he believed his basic job was simply to help people name their soul experiences; in other words, to help others interpret the depth of their living. Pastors who assist the interpretative communications of others deal ultimately with matters of the spirit.

EVALUATIVE COMMUNICATION

In *Psychotherapy and the Christian Message*, Albert C. Outler sums up his specific outlook: "All that is distinctively and specifically *human* about our lives focuses on this mystery of self-involved decision about the right and the good—the choice of ends proper to our selfhood and the choice of means appropriate to our chosen ends."[5] Outler gives particular emphasis to the centrality of what we call evaluative communication— the inclination to declare values, pronounce judgments, and espouse virtue-directed behavior. We take a stand. We assert that one outcome is more important than another outcome. We propose that one course of action is more ethical than another. We claim that certain behavior is appropriate or inappropriate. We rate ourselves and others according to values we deem significant.

Any event or issue can be approached using evaluative communication. When a search committee must decide between two candidates, evaluative communication can be central to the process. The members can discuss who of the two has more quality as a person, who seems less like a person of God, whose faith seems more genuine. Pragmatic communication ("Can we afford him?"), feeling communication ("I was more comfortable with her"), and interpretative communication ("We're probably biased toward male ministers in our denomination") can inform the final decision, but evaluative communication regarding selecting a candidate who meets certain standards can be dominant.

A common tendency of people engaged in evaluative communication is absolutism. People are very touchy about their values. While their values may change, they maintain a degree of absoluteness about whatever value system they have at any given time, along with a degree of rage when those values are questioned. The more vulnerable individuals become, the more difficulty they have living with ambiguity or plurality of values.

Evaluative communication is vital as it *helps anchor our self-esteem.* We deem ourselves special when we attach ourselves to principles that inspire us. We weather blows to our self by leaning on cherished ideals. Our pictures of what is right and wrong carry our sense of worth.

Evaluative communication helps anchor our identity. Firm identity and fidelity to values go hand in hand. What we declare we stand for solidifies for us who we are. A popular hymn proclaims this truth: "They will know we are Christians by our love." Similarly we know who we are by the values we enact. Evaluative communication constantly shores up the boundaries of our identity. When evaluative communication is weak, that is, when our expressed values are weak, we tend to lose our character—in other words, to lose our moral stance in life as well as the definition of who we are.

Evaluative communication anchors us in community. Shared values are the glue of groups. We experience our deepest sense of belonging when we are with kindred spirits who embody similar values. Evaluative communication expresses as well as reaffirms our communal membership. When evaluative communication is absent, communities deteriorate. Isolation and anomie arise.

Clergy who help parishioners with their evaluative communications are doing more than values clarification. They are helping others with life clarification. Selfhood itself, along with its proper ends and means, is being formed.

Types of Evaluative Communication:
Affirming and Critical

Throughout this chapter we have been describing the general nature of each communication form. Each is complex in ways we have not tried to analyze. For our pastoral work, however, we need to highlight two particular forms of evaluative communication: affirming and critical.

Each evaluative comment tends to have some mixture of affirming coloration and critical coloration. Evaluative communication that is affirming ranges from mere compliments about persons, objects, or events to adoring praise of them. Evaluative communication with critical overtones ranges from slightly dissatisfied comments to vilifying castigations.

Human relationships are shaped by the presence, intensity, and dominance of affirming or critical evaluative communication. In the following chapters when I refer simply to critical evaluative communication, I am referring to an acute or chronic pervasiveness of this form over the other. Similarly, references to affirming evaluative communication emphasize the dominance of this form over critical evaluative communication.

Determining whether evaluative communication is mostly critical or affirming may be difficult, however. A parent's scolding of a child is critical but may not be completely negative. A layperson's congratulations to a pastor is affirming but may not be completely positive. The following discussion oversimplifies the complexity regarding evaluative communication, but it gives pastors conceptual tools to use in working with couples, groups, and individuals.

In some situations, affirming and critical evaluative communication are balanced. Both sides of an issue are valued, as shown in these examples: "The children should not be in adult worship and yet they should be there"; "a woman has a right to chose abortion and yet she should not destroy life." More commonly, however, balanced evaluative communication expresses an equal amount of both critical evaluative communication and affirming evaluative communication. One spouse who complained about the insensitivity of the partner at a party also simultaneously praised the partner's usually good tact: "You're often very attuned to things, but that night you blew it!" One pastor called this balance of critical and affirming evaluative communication "nice bitching."

Other communications reveal mixed proportions of affirming and critical evaluative coloration. For example, the level of affirming evaluative coloration begins slightly to exceed critical evaluative coloration in a case where a pastor's affirmation may be of a mild nature, such as saying simply in a council meeting, "That was a good suggestion, Tom."

The intensification of the affirming coloration with a corresponding decrease in expressed, implied, or assume critical coloration may be evident if the same pastor's communication regarding Tom becomes more emphatic, such as saying in front of the gathered congregation, "Tom's work has blessed us tremendously."

The pastor's affirming evaluative communication regarding Tom may become intensely idealized, with critical evaluative communication about Tom's humanness essentially nonexistent, if he or she were to say, "Tom is absolutely marvelous! If we do whatever he tells us, he'll turn things around for us."

Affirming evaluative communication is constructive for the most part. People grow under the glow of praise. But excesses can be detrimental. Unchecked adulation can lead individuals to mistrust the affirmation they receive, to act with grandiosity, or to put themselves in jeopardy. In counseling, for example, I call into question the elaborate praise a woman heaps on an abusive husband. Her idealizing comments may be an attempt to ward off the pain of what she is going through—"He really didn't mean it. He's a wonderful husband and father"—but it leaves her vulnerable to further assaults on body and soul.

While we might hope that an aura of affirming evaluative communication can infuse our interpretative, feeling, and pragmatic communications, in the extreme it can also contaminate the other forms. Idealized communication regarding a partner can so bias interpretative communication that only one perspective is expressed. Similarly, feeling communication may become restricted to a narrow band of affect, namely allowing only positive emotions to surface. Likewise, pragmatic communication may be narrowed to a single aim.

For instance, a woman in therapy with me asked me to write a letter on behalf of her husband who was "in a little trouble"—he had been convicted and jailed on charges ranging from mail fraud to selling drugs. She had suffered greatly in her relationship with him, but she pleaded how good a man he was (affirming evaluative communication). That excessive affirmation, however, contaminated her interpretative communication: "Really, it isn't all or much of his fault." It contaminated her feeling communication: "All I have in my heart is concern for him." It also contaminated her pragmatic communication: "There is only one thing to do—get him out."

Critical evaluative communication, conversely, can also dominate relationships. Reprimanding someone for his or her "own good," for example, reveals a state in which the level of critical evaluative coloration begins to exceed affirming evaluative coloration. To cite another example, a lay leader of a stewardship committee delivered these comments to the congregation: "If we do everything just for institutional survival, it won't work! God's ways work, not the ways of the world! What we *really* mean when we say, 'We are giving all we can,' is 'We are giving all we choose to give at this time.' That is not God's way!" His words were evaluative communication; he was speaking of what "ought" to happen. But more specifically his words were critical evaluative communication as he was calling into question the behavior of others, invoking a higher value, namely God's way, and demeaning the ways of the world as lesser values doomed to failure.

Interpreting his words as critical evaluative communication says nothing about the condition of his heart. Inwardly he may deeply love the people he addresses, and his words may be intended for their well-being. Neither does this interpretation indicate that his words were inappropriate or would be unwelcome to those who heard him.

As critical evaluative communication intensifies, however, specific individuals, groups, or events become less and less affirmed. In the following statement, for example, an increase in critical coloration corresponds with a diminishment of affirming coloration: "Gays and lesbians are God's children, but because of their sinful lifestyle they should not be allowed as members of a regular church."

At the extreme, critical evaluative communication contains vitriolic denouncements. "How she is acting toward me is totally unforgivable," stated an enraged husband. "I hope she rots in hell!" "Until the church president resigns we won't come to worship," asserted some members to their pastor. "He is nothing but mean-spirited and self-centered. He should not only resign, but should be told to leave." "I am worthless, useless, no good to anyone," commented an individual. Affirmative evaluative communication in these instances is nil, and the potential for such is negligible.

Some degree of critical evaluative communication can be helpful to others, but it is usually counterproductive when it dominates. The self-esteem of couples, groups, and individuals deteriorates under the lash of criticism. In my counseling work, I regularly urge, even require, persons to stop their verbal attacks on others or themselves. "You may not like yourself, but at least stop calling yourself names," I say to self-flagellating individuals, for example. In some situations, however, what looks like critical evaluative communication may be therapeutic. A person may verbally attack another individual in an effort figuratively to awaken him or her, for example, but this is more in the framework of pragmatic communication than critical evaluative communication.

Pastors also need to recognize differences between critical evaluative communication and feeling communication that involves anger. First, anger expressed as feeling communication is owned more as one's own experience, and second, it is used more for being understood than forcing compliance. If the enraged husband above had been engaged in feeling communication he might have said, "I feel totally betrayed by her. I'm devastated! Something inside me wishes that something horrible would happen to her. It hurts bad." Persons expressing anger often jump back and forth between these forms of communication, or have their feeling communication contaminated by covert critical evaluative expressions.

HOW COMMUNICATION FORMS INTERACT

No pure form of communication exists. Any interpretative comment always involves a value judgment, a feeling component, and pragmatic implications. Pragmatic dialogue always includes underlying feelings, interpretations, and evaluations. People often move rapidly between various forms of communication even within the same verbal paragraph.

Nonetheless, some distinctions do exist, and certain forms predominate. Subject matter, current situations, or personal habit may induce the dominant use of a certain form. Crises, for example, tend to make people revert to a form of communication that represents security. They momentarily lose the flexibility of communicating on various levels as they establish a holding pattern centered around a single communication form. Similarly, when parishioners find themselves in a group where one form of communication is subtly mandated, they tend to assume that communication form. If a church group is immersed in feeling communication, without reflecting on those feelings (without interpretative communication), without discussion of what to do with those feelings (without pragmatic communication), or without judging the merits of what they are saying (without evaluative communication), new participants frequently suspend their normal range of communication approaches as they assume the group's dominant feeling communication form.

Individuals also develop the habit of using one form of communication predominantly. For example, one woman with a pragmatic orientation spoke matter-of-factly about the situations in life she had to face:

"After school I had to work because our family was poor. I did odd jobs, and worked my way up. By the time I was sixteen I was totally supporting myself and half of the family. That's the way it was." Someone else might have spoken with more feeling about such circumstances.

While there is no inherent hierarchical order in the forms of communication, individuals may establish personal hierarchical arrangements. Another individual also met every situation by first trying to decide how to handle it (he made pragmatic communication predominant). When that failed, his second approach was to announce what he stood for (evaluative communication). His next step, entered into reluctantly but often out of necessity, was to try to understand what went wrong (interpretative communication). The final step, which was last because it was most difficult for him, was to express what was inside him (feeling communication). Recognizing the hierarchical arrangement of a couple, group, or individual's use of communication forms can aid in our pastoral interventions.

ary and Harold Teel arrive for the appointment they have made with their pastor, Reverend Sims. They enter his office looking sullen.

Mrs. Teel: We're not communicating well at all. He just doesn't listen to me. I try to tell him my feelings about problems at my job, but all he does is tell me what I ought to do about them.

Reverend Sims (to Mrs. Teel): Are you coming today then, Mary, to work on your communication?

Mrs. Teel: Yes.

Reverend Sims: Do you want to work on communicating your feelings about your job, or to work on the breakdown in your communication?

Mrs. Teel: Both. We don't communicate well, and that's especially upsetting when something important comes up.

Reverend Sims (to Mr. Teel): And what do you want to talk about today, Harold?

Mr. Teel: You two go on. I'll just listen. *(He sits back with a perturbed look on his face.)*

Reverend Sims (to Mr. Teel after sitting reflectively for a few moments): Perhaps the communication between you two has become so frustrating that it seems the only thing you can do is stop talking.

Mr. Teel nods silently.

Every minister has encountered couples like this. Their communication is stuck, and the longer it stays stuck, the more distant they become. Getting them to talk again is helpful, but getting them to talk in a new way is crucial. Communication-oriented pastors like Reverend Sims are attentive to these communication impasses. If the couple indicates that communication is the problem, or if, after observation, the pastor assesses that communication problems are primary, the pastor will focus counseling on the couple's communication.

Reverend Sims demonstrated from the outset his commitment to test out the possibility that communication problems were *causes* of relational difficulties rather than mere *expressions* of them. The problems couples present may need approaches other than communication counseling, but pastors can develop the routine of assessing whether communication difficulties are primary or secondary. Taking a clue from Mrs. Teel's opening statement, Reverend Sims sought to clarify whether she really did intend to work on communication issues. From Mr. Teel's withdrawal, Reverend Sims began to assess whether communication difficulties were pivotal for him. These and other responses from Mr. and Mrs. Teel would determine whether communication should be central in their counseling.

Reverend Sims's responses also suggested his basic communication approach in working with couples. His question to Mrs. Teel was an encouragement of pragmatic communication ("Are you coming today then, Mary, to work . . ."). His comment to Mr. Teel was an encouragement of interpretative communication ("Perhaps the communication between you . . ."). Interpretative and pragmatic communication would be the key forms from which he would work if communication problems were primary.

From the stance of interpretative communication, he would *teach* them about their communication patterns and problems, and then, from the stance of pragmatic communication, he would *coach* them in practicing new ways of communicating. Aiding their communication would be the major means for aiding their relationship. Even if communication problems were not primary for Mr. and Mrs. Teel, Reverend Sims could use teaching and coaching about communication as a valuable auxiliary approach.

COMMON COMMUNICATION PROBLEMS FOR COUPLES

When spouses talk, each operates from a particular form of communication. Each implicitly expects that the other spouse will recognize that form and respond in a like manner. When the other spouse responds from a different form of communication, however, the relationship becomes disturbed. The couple may then talk about what has gone wrong with their communication (interpretative communication), about what is going on inside them (feeling communication), or about how they should handle this situation (pragmatic communication).

Often, unfortunately, they regress to critical evaluative communication, which may dominate affirming evaluative communication either temporarily or chronically. Accusations and put-downs also replace reflection and problem solving, as happened with the Teels. Their case illustrates two common communication problems for couples: operating from different forms of communication, and regressing to critical evaluative communication.

Operating from Different Forms of Communication

In the following conversation, Mr. and Mrs. Teel are operating from different forms of communication. Mrs. Teel relates from the feeling communication mode. The expression of her feelings, and Mr. Teel's resonating with those feelings, are what she wants. She may have capacities for pragmatic communication, and she may respond at times from the level of interpretative communication, but at this point she grounds herself in feeling communication.

Mr. Teel relates to his wife with pragmatic communication. Looking at things concretely and coming up with solutions is the approach he takes to her expressions of troubled feelings. He may have capacities for interpretative communication, and he may react at times from the level of feeling communication, but in this instance he roots himself in pragmatic communication.

Mrs. Teel: All I want him to do is just listen to how I feel about things at work. It would also be nice if he expressed some compassion for what I'm going through there. But he just keeps telling me the best way to handle the situation. He acts like he's supervising one of his employees rather than talking to his wife!

Mr. Teel: I'm just trying to help. I know she's having trouble, but finding solutions to the problems seems not only the logical thing to do but also the best way for me to help her. But when she keeps saying that my suggestions aren't what she wants, I tell her to deal with it herself.

This feeling-pragmatic mismatch is a common cause of marital stress. One partner wants the comfort of feeling communication. The other offers pragmatic communication. Neither party is wrong; their approaches simply fail to correspond to what the other expects—and needs. If the spouses are not *able* to make alterations in their communication forms, then personality limitations may be present. For instance, if Mr. Teel can relate to people only from a pragmatic level, he may suffer from a psychological disorder. If the spouses are not *willing* to alter their communication forms, however, then they likely have regressed to the fortress of critical evaluative communication.

Operating from different forms of communication may work for couples on a short-term basis. Mrs. Teel may find reassurance, at times, in a pragmatic husband whom she knows will not become upset with her emotions. Mr. Teel may find relief, at times, in a wife who vicariously expresses for him feelings he is apprehensive of showing. When habitual, however, his pragmatic communication becomes irritating to her, and her feeling communication becomes frustrating to him.

Feeling-interpretative mismatches also produce tension. One partner may communicate from the feeling level while the other does so from the interpretative level. One husband just wanted to "let my feelings flow and have them listened to" (feeling communication). When his wife offered her different opinion about the content of his feeling (interpretative communication), he experienced great dismay. Similarly, one wife wanted her husband to express feelings for her situation twenty years ago which he could not resonate with then. He was uneasy, and unpracticed, in feeling communication, and offered interpretative communication instead: "It must have been very hard for you then." She brushed aside this objectification of her feelings: "I want you to tell me how it would feel *if you were me* in that situation, not make *comments* about how I might have felt."

This same feeling-interpretative mismatch happens in other relationships. For example, a person may join a Bible study group expecting it to be a learning situation (interpretative communication). The group, however, may center most of its time expressing personal problems (feeling communication).

Pragmatic-interpretative mismatches are likewise disruptive. One spouse is ready for action, and pragmatic communication is asked for, if not demanded: "We've got to decided one way or the other. Time is running out." The other spouse, however, may still be immersed in interpretative communication: "We have to understand what all this means first. We have to make sense of this before we act." Interpretative communication seems like avoidance to the pragmatic communicator. Pragmatic communication seems like impulsiveness to the interpretative communicator.

An *evaluative-interpretative mismatch* can disturb relationships as well. One husband tended to speak of every event in terms of the values central to him (evaluative communication), while his wife tended to speak of the various factors that may have contributed to the event (interpretative communication). Her failure to communicate as a moral advocate left him disillusioned with her. His failure to communicate as an understanding human being left her lonely for companionship.

A specific evaluative-pragmatic mismatch also generates discord, namely an *affirming evaluative-pragmatic mismatch*. One woman had been taught by her mother to always say something nice about a person.

In her marriage, consequently, she tended to communicate in an affirming evaluative form, even when a situation called for an alternative response. When differences of opinion arose with her husband, she showered the moment with testimonies of his goodness and the wonderfulness of their marriage. Her husband, however, tried to establish pragmatic conversation that would resolve their differences. His issue communication left her feeling unaffirmed. Her "warm fuzzies" communication left him feeling frustrated.

This mismatch may happen in church groups. Council members may look for strong administrative leadership from their pastor. They may expect him or her to operate primarily from the pragmatic form of communication. The pastor, however, may be inclined to stroke people with compliments and praise. His or her primary mode of communication may be affirming evaluative rather than pragmatic. The council members may become intolerant of the pastor's backslapping, while the pastor may become irritated with their functionalism.

Operating from different forms of communication accounts for the majority of initial relationship problems. The communication-oriented pastor will wisely look for these problems first in working with couples, groups, and individuals.

Regressing to Critical Evaluative Communication

When communication mismatches continue, couples frequently move from their initial form of communication to critical evaluative communication. Affirming evaluative communication may be present or implied, but manifestations of critical evaluative communication prevail.

At times, critical evaluative communication may be the only form existing between the couple. Pragmatic, feeling, and interpretative communications basically vanish. "We're at war," said one husband. "We hit each other where it hurts whenever we can."

Most often, however, other forms of communication continue to exist but are contaminated by critical evaluative communication. A couple's attempts to inflict injury are carried by the other forms of communication: pragmatic, feeling, and interpretative. As a result, these other forms become poisoned by the couple's critical evaluative communication, and they lose their power to facilitate daily living or to nurture relationships. For example, a wife wanted to talk to her resentful husband about altering plans for picking up the children after school. The husband's pragmatic communication was contaminated by his underlying critical evaluative communication: "We agreed that you would pick them up on Tuesday and Thursday. This is Thursday." His cold pragmatic conversation, adhering to the letter rather than the spirit of the law, carried his hostility.

Mr. and Mrs. Teel also moved to critical evaluative communication. As Mrs. Teel continued to talk about how she felt, and Mr. Teel continued to talk about what should be done, those communications were used to channel critical communication. The foreground sounded like feeling communication and pragmatic communication, but the background was critical evaluative communication.

Contamination of pragmatic communication is ubiquitous in divorce cases. Supposedly practical discussions about property settlements, visitation rights, and child support payments are replete with underlying critical evaluative sentiments. Clarifying the contamination of pragmatic communication does not eliminate critical communication for couples. It does, however, work toward restoring pragmatic communication so that at least the minimal needs of people can be met.

Contamination of interpretative communication likewise perpetuates marital stress. When a wife says to her husband, "You're just like your father," she is making more than an interpretation. A knife is cloaked in that comment. When a husband says, "She has ups and downs in her moods like a crazy woman," he is making more than an interpretation. A rock is being hurled. These two interpretations may contain truth, but the critical evaluative communication beneath infects how the interpretation is made and how it is received.

Feeling communication may also be compromised by critical evaluative communication. The hostile spouse who condemns the partner may claim that he or she is "only expressing my feelings." Assertions that one has a right to one's feelings are also used to justify venomous comments. The role of feelings as a means for understanding is thereby compromised.

Couples are not always aware of this contamination of their communication. When Reverend Sims asked Mr. and Mrs. Teel about their attacks on each other, they were surprised at this interpretation. "I'm just expressing my feelings," claimed Mrs. Teel. "I'm just stating what should be done," asserted Mr. Teel.

Other couples normalize the contamination. For example, couples who fight about every decision as part of their problem solving may claim this is regular communication. "It's a part of our culture," they may say, or, "That's how our parents did it, and they were married for fifty years." Asserting the normalcy of contaminated communication diminishes awareness of its destructive power.

Couples may also succumb to critical evaluative communication as its own justification. Viewing the other partner as the enemy sets up new standards and expanded options for action. Couples may feel entitled to defend themselves. Any show of "weakness" may be considered leaving oneself vulnerable to further attack. Claims of doing this for someone's own good support one's "doing whatever it takes." Critical evaluative communication fosters self-justifications.

With empathic teaching, however, couples are able to perceive the contamination in their daily communication. They are also able quickly to understand how they operate from different forms of communication. Recognition of these behaviors often relieves the tensions between the couple. Coaching them toward the establishment of decontaminated communication and compatible forms of communication takes longer. The reward, however, is an enhancement of the couple's life together.

APPROACHES FOR CAREGIVERS

When the relationship between a couple is fragmenting, they yearn for something that will glue them back together. Fear of total collapse tends to inspire frantic communication or communication withdrawal—neither of which is therapeutic. When a pastor begins to communicate interpretatively and pragmatically to the couple, they experience a sense of relief. A promise of order is brought into their lives. The pastor's teaching bestows meaning on their relationship. The pastor's coaching restores cooperation in their relationship.

Using Interpretative Communication to Teach

After a pastor has established that communication difficulties are primary and has assessed the nature of those difficulties, he or she can proceed from an interpretative communication framework. This process, which can begin even in the first meeting with the couple, will involve first teaching them the four forms of communication, and then teaching them about their own unique communication problems.

To simplify the teaching process, I recommend using an easel, preferably one with large sheets of paper. The couple is helped by viewing together the diagrams the pastor will draw, rather than looking at separate pages handed to them. Standing in front of the easel, the pastor focuses attention on the learning process and elicits from the couple their reflection rather than their fighting.

I typically begin by stating that communication seems to be their central or immediate problem. That, I say, needs to be looked at right away. I indicate that the amount of communication is not as important as the type of communication in leading to marital trouble. Going to the easel, I draw a box with four levels, like the one in the introduction. Above it I write "Forms of Communication." I then turn to the couple and say, "There are four basic forms of communication. Whenever people communicate to each other, no matter where they are, they speak from one of these forms. Marriage partners, for example, communicate to each other in these four ways. We can also think of these forms as being like frames of mind. When we communicate from one of these forms, we are in that frame of mind."

I ask them if I'm making things clear so far. If not, I try again. When questions about "Why are we doing this?" arise, I rephrase an explanation about the issue I hear them bringing to me, namely how their relationship is suffering because their communication is suffering. I persevere with the teaching in spite of the anger the couple may have toward each other. In fact, the more hostility the couple shows, the more a structured communication approach is required.

Next, I write the word *pragmatic* in the bottom level and explain pragmatic communication using the basic explanations and examples from chapter 1. I then do the same for feeling, interpretative, and evaluative communication. I also use examples that I pick up from the couple themselves. I might say to a wife: "When you commented that it may be hard for both of you to express your feelings when you fear being hurt, that was interpretative communication. It certainly had some feeling behind it, but it was an interpretation about what motivated your behavior." This helps the couple begin to identify the various communication forms and to make important distinctions between them.

I also use the couple's responses to my routine question, "What comes to your mind about these forms of communication?" I do not focus on the content of their answers, but on the form of communication they employ. For example, I may say to a husband, "When you said that it was sad that you two had not understood this about your communication years ago, that was feeling communication. You were communicating how you were feeling about your relationship with your partner right now, namely, sad for the both of you." Once again, the effort is to help them understand the forms of communication and to see how in the present moment they are expressing one form or another.

If the couple catches on quickly, I may teach through quizzing. I may say to a wife, "You just commented that you thought of a way to use this communication approach with your children. What form of communication were you in when you said that? What was your communicative frame of mind?" She should recognize this as pragmatic communication because she was thinking of applicability and problem solving.

In an effort to foster understanding of a couple's communication problems, a pastor can begin to teach through crossover questions. Using this means, the pastor also teaches the importance of two interpretative questions: "From what communication form am I operating?" and "From what communication form is my partner operating?"

Reverend Sims (to Mr. Teel): When Mary wanted to talk to you about what was going on at her job, what form of communication do you think she was operating from?

Mr. Teel: Well, in light of what we're talking about, I suppose she was in feeling communication.

Reverend Sims (to Mrs. Teel): Is that how you would interpret where you were, Mary?

Mrs. Teel: Yes.

Reverend Sims (to Mr. Teel): And did Mary stay in that form of communication?

Mr. Teel: No. She became frustrated with me. She began to put me down. She moved into what you call critical evaluative communication.

Reverend Sims (to Mrs. Teel): Did it seem that was the form of communication you slipped into?

Mrs. Teel: No. I felt that I was still just expressing my feelings. But I can begin to see how a lot of negativity started to enter into what I said to Harold.

Reverend Sims (to Mrs. Teel): What form of communication was Harold in, Mary, when he started to talk to you about your job?

Mrs. Teel: He was in pragmatic communication, but I didn't want him to be. He's always in that mode. He never listens to me!

Reverend Sims (to Mrs. Teel): The last part of your comment was critical evaluative communication, wasn't it? What we're trying to do now is stay in interpretative communication. That will help us in the long run. So, you interpret that Harold was in pragmatic communication at the beginning?

Mrs. Teel: Yes.

Reverend Sims (to Mr. Teel): Is that your interpretation, Harold? Were you operating from the pragmatic form of communication?

Mr. Teel: Yes, I was.

Reverend Sims (to Mrs. Teel): Did Harold stay in that form of communication, Mary?

Mrs. Teel: No. Like me he went into critical evaluative communication.

Reverend Sims (to Mr. Teel): Is that the form you slipped into, Harold?

Mr. Teel: Well, like Mary, I'd like to think not. I'd like to think I was simply backing off, pragmatically. But a coldness did enter what I said to her after that. I'd have to make the interpretation that I did move to critical evaluative communication to a certain extent.

Reverend Sims (to both of them): And what happened when you both started communicating basically from the critical evaluative level?

Mr. Teel: Things just got worse and worse. It seemed we couldn't talk about anything without there being an edge to it. We weren't calling each other names, but we certainly were put out with each other.

Mrs. Teel: The communication became so frustrating that we finally called you for help.

Reverend Sims: So, we have a pretty clear picture of what went wrong. When your forms of communication did not match, and each of you was not able to get the other person to change to yours, then your relationship became strained. After a time you regressed to evaluative communication, especially in the form of critical evaluative communication. Once there, it was hard for both of you to escape, as it often is for couples.

A pastor will need to walk a couple through their communication problem several times by using different instances they remember. Different types of communication mismatches may also become evident. All the while the pastor operates basically from interpretative communication, and encourages the couple to do the same. The stage is then set for pragmatic communication in the form of coaching.

Using Pragmatic Communication to Coach

My coaching efforts with couples typically involve using pragmatic communication to minimize the contaminating effects of critical evaluative communication and to encourage the development of alternative communication forms. Initial efforts to halt critical evaluative communication are necessary when it manifests itself markedly in a couple's relationship. Then coaching on how to enhance a communication form, or how to develop communication forms other than their habitual ones, can follow.

Although I work primarily with couples from the stance of interpretative and pragmatic communication, affirming evaluative communication is an important adjunct. By acknowledging their insights and praising their efforts, I sustain the couple in the hard work of communication change. Furthermore, by allowing time for the couple's feeling communication, without asking them about the communication process, I convey understanding for their need to have someone "just know how I feel." Interpretative and pragmatic communication remain central, however.

When couples have regressed to critical evaluative communication, or when their other communication forms have been markedly contaminated by that form, I direct the couple to do two things: (1) raise the white flag (call a truce), and (2) relate only through pragmatic communication.

Critical evaluative communication can leave an impression on one's interpretative communication. Hostile words of criticism begin to form into an interpretation that, "He really sees me that way," or, "She really is that kind of person." One begins to think that the negativity of the other partner is his or her real personality, rather than just how he or she responds when scared or hurt. Raising the white flag is a crisis measure to minimize contamination of interpretative communication. "Your critical evaluative communication is dangerous," I tell them. "It not only draws blood, it also infects your future. If nothing else, you need to stop the verbal attacks on each other. Mutually agree to raise the white flag."

In an effort to minimize critical evaluative communication and its effects, I also coach them to relate only through pragmatic communication. I may say to them, "It would be nice to be able to express your feelings, but you are both so tender with each other that those feelings could be easily misunderstood, and further explosions would likely happen. Trying to make interpretations to each other may be safer than expressing feelings, but that level of communication is also vulnerable. The same is true about evaluative communication. So for a while, just stay on the pragmatic level. Your communication should be about practical decisions and arrangements you need to make to keep your day organized."

One couple, heavily into critical evaluative communication, tried to elicit promises from each other and signs of the other's respect. These are valid requests, but they are goals rather than fundamental starting points for conflicted couples. What is needed at first are pragmatic arrangements rather than promises, working plans rather than nebulous signs of respect. Coaching for pragmatic communication also minimizes guilt and unilateral decisions since it stresses mutual involvement.

I next turn to coaching on communication forms, although decontamination continues as this coaching begins. Getting the couples to practice using different communication forms is a staple of communication counseling. For example, I'll ask a husband what form he wants to communicate in regarding a certain subject, and then I'll coach him to speak in that communicative form. If he slips into interpretative communication when he is trying to be in feeling communication, I will stop him, indicate that he is in interpretative communication, and identify the marks of interpretative communication verses feeling communication.

I may also model for one of the spouses the form of communication the other spouse needs. I may say: "Your wife seems to be looking for affirming evaluative communication. She may want to hear something like, 'You deserve to have a good time after all the problems we've been having.'" I will then turn to the spouse to see if both the communication form and its particular way of being expressed are on target.

The content of these exchanges during office practice becomes secondary. I focus more on how things are being said than on what is being said. The content has usually been rehashed scores of times by the couple. What needs to be changed is their communication about that content. As a result, the content usually changes, too. New data emerge, or old data are understood in a new way.

Marriage partners may also need help learning to communicate in forms basically foreign to them in order to break patterns of using certain communication forms habitually. Conversations often become routinized as most talk is routed through a person's habitual communication form, and certain statements and lines become routine responses to whatever occurs. Such communication patterns dictate thought, feeling, and behavior.

For example, the communication of one vulnerable couple was severely restricted. She would respond to everything using interpretative communication. He would respond to everything with evaluative communication. She would interpret whatever happened, and he would judge it. Each had heard the other's habitual responses so often that they no longer even asked what the other thought. Little novelty or growth entered their relationship. This routinization of their communication also served the purpose of avoiding feeling communication, which for them was not only foreign but also dangerous. Emerging feelings were routed through their habitual communication forms: she would veil her feelings in interpretations, and he would veil his feelings in evaluations.

In our counseling, I directed them to take turns speaking, each for five straight minutes, from the level of feeling communication. The listening spouse was not to interrupt, but to adopt the feeling communication orientation and resonate with the speaker's feelings. This approach sought to enhance their feeling communication in two ways: by initiating them into expression of self-owned feelings, and by strengthening their capacities for resonant feelings, that is, being in tune with the feelings of the other.

It was hard for them to do. She would start with a feeling but slip quickly into an interpretative mode. To assist her, I suggested she think of concentric circles, like a bull's-eye target. I asked her: "If the circles were layers of feeling communication, what on the outside would be the easiest feelings to talk about? What next, on the next inside ring, would be the feelings somewhat harder to talk about, and what next, on the inside ring, would be the hardest feelings to talk about?" She identified each layer, and we worked for a long time on feeling communication at the least threatening level.

Because the husband had a tendency simply to respond to whatever his wife said rather than getting in touch with his own feelings, I directed him to begin the five-minute focus by expressing his feelings. He, too, struggled with this. I suggested that he practice communicating self-owned feelings by keeping a journal, by paying attention to his felt sense of things, and by watching how others related through feeling communication.

Homework is also a staple of communication counseling. For example, I will direct the couple to be very deliberate when talking at home. A husband should say, "I'm making an interpretation now," if that is the communication mode he has chosen. If his wife hears his communication differently than he intended, by responding to him with pragmatic communication, for instance, then he should say, "I wasn't communicating on the pragmatic level. I was trying to communicate interpretatively."

I also give an example of what not to do, namely respond with critical evaluative communication. I will say to the husband, "When your wife doesn't meet your need to have her respond with interpretative communication, don't say, 'You just don't understand!' That's moving toward critical evaluative communication. Say instead, 'You haven't quite got the point I'm trying to make. I'm trying to communicate from the interpretative level.'"

I also suggest to the couple that if they are not able to join each other in some common communication form, or if they begin to regress to critical evaluative communication, they should revert to pragmatic communication. In doing this, they should overtly announce to each other that they are moving to the pragmatic communication form.

This open labeling and pronouncement to the other of one's communication form may feel stilted. "I shouldn't have to explain," said one wife. "He should know already." I respond interpretatively to such statements: "When persons have broken legs they need crutches until their legs heal, and when a couple's communication is broken, they need crutches, too, until they heal." In addition, I will often move to affirming evaluative communication and say, "I know this is hard, but you can do it. You're worth it and your marriage is worth it."

Teaching about communication forms and communication problems can productively happen in other settings. Within churches I have taught women's circles, youth groups, and retired men's fellowships about communication forms. Outside the local church I have taught clergy groups and denominational staffs about communication forms and communication problems stemming from them. The explanations are usually quickly understood. Even without personal coaching, those who hear begin to envision what changes could and should be made. When that happens, pastors are once again touching the very quick of peoples' lives.

A newly formed search committee had been assigned the task of screening candidates for the position of associate minister, the church's first staff addition. A job description and required qualifications had been provided by the pastor and the church council. Selected candidates were to be considered later by an expanded committee. The congregation as a whole supported the project. The search committee's first meeting convened with an air of excitement.

By the end of the fourth meeting, several members made an appointment with the pastor. "We're not getting anywhere," stated one individual. "We started out all right, but then our communication fell apart. We can't seem to find common ground. Now the tension is so high that several people are threatening to leave the committee. We need your help."

Church groups often have trouble with their communication. Our usual pastoral response is to consider the group's composition rather than its communication. But just as communication can *shape* a couple's relationship as well as be a symptom of other problems, so, too, can communication be a *determiner* of a group's relationships as well as an indicator of its relationships. When pastors recognize that communication problems are central to the difficulties within groups, then a communication approach can be taken to guide them. Even when communication is secondary rather than primary, a communication approach can be used as an auxiliary aid.

Once again, I am not suggesting that all problems can be solved simply by altering communication patterns. But I am confident that a pastoral approach to communication problems can aid healing and stimulate growth. In this chapter I describe two basic types of communication problems in church groups and pastoral approaches that can be used to deal with these problems.

Communication and group cohesion go hand in hand. Communication in a group both reflects and shapes a group's cohesion. In certain instances, communication tends to become a primary means by which cohesion is established. For example, when a group is being formed, the nature of its communication serves as the initial bonding agent. Parishioners who have recently lost a loved one share a similar experience, but they begin to coalesce as a group as their communication draws them together. When they communicate on the same wavelength (that is, when they find a common communication form), the group develops a sense of commonality and care. If the group lacks a central, organizing communication form, however, it remains a collection of isolated individuals. Group organization often develops from repeated use of a common communication form. Group diffusion often exists when the group fails to congeal around a central communication form. Pastors recognize the importance of this, for in a newly forming group we try to "keep the conversation flowing" and "keep the conversation on track."

Communication also serves as group glue when its cohesion is threatened. For instance, when a church feels endangered by outside forces, that church may defend itself by intensifying its internal communication efforts. Revival of group communication becomes a means for closing ranks, and focused communication draws clear battle lines. The church may declare more emphatically its special understanding of God's will (interpretative communication). It may sharpen its condemnation of particular moral evils in society (evaluative communication). It may expand on plans for bringing in new members (pragmatic communication). It may incite expressions of the community's fear, grief, or anger (feeling communication). Rhetoric intensifies in proportion to vulnerability. Galvanized communication becomes a means for galvanizing the group.

Communication and group identity also go hand in hand. Communication both reflects and shapes a group's identity. How a group talks, however, may be the primary determiner of its identity. We have

already spoken of how a newly formed Bible study group may find itself
slipping consistently and heavily into feeling communication. That form
may become the unspoken expectation as to how the group will communicate. Feeling communication may become the currency of influence
and acceptance. People who come into the group may feel pressured to
communicate in the group way or else be left out.

In summary, forms of communication provide the fundamental
resources groups use for developing cohesion, defining identity, and establishing group process. Communication is not the only resource, of course,
but it is a coagulating agent often underappreciated if not unrecognized.

The groups discussed in this chapter are those with which we pastors
have formal working relationships. *Standing groups* include those established by the church's constitution or central to the church's structure,
such as the consistory (session, council), membership committee, worship committee, Christian education committee, and finance committee.
Special task groups include those installed for specific time-limited functions, such as a search committee, constitution revision committee, ren-
ovation committee, and anniversary committee. *Activity groups* include
those gathered for fellowship, service, and/or learning, such as a Bible
study group, bereavement group, new parent group, retired men's group,
and women's circle. Pastors come in contact with a host of informal and
ad hoc groups that they are not in a position to guide. This chapter
focuses on the communication problems of established church groups
with whom clergy most often interact.

COMMON COMMUNICATION PROBLEMS FOR GROUPS

Church groups may exhibit one of two basic communication problems.
First, some groups suffer from the lack of a central communication form
that would bind them into a cohesive unit. This frequently occurs in
newly formed groups, but it can also be a chronic problem of long-stand-
ing groups. Communication within such groups is uncoordinated.

Progress is impaired. Without the stabilization provided by a central communication form, conflicts often surface between members, as evident in the search committee example at the beginning of this chapter. Without group stability provided by a central communication form, these conflicts can escalate.

Second, some groups suffer from rigidity of a central communication form. The group operates from a hardened communication style that gives it structure but of a restricted nature. Other forms of communication are either expelled or absorbed into the rigid central communication form. Work in the group may proceed, but within narrowed boundaries. True interchange with other groups is limited. Those individuals who fail to adopt the group's dominant communication form lack power or even the possibility of membership.

Other groups are blessed with a central and flexible communication form. Here members still retain their individuality and personal communication inclinations, but a central communication form helps establish group cohesiveness. When stabilized around the structure of a central communication form, the group is able to utilize the other communication forms in productive ways. These other forms may also be made central on a short-term basis, or the group can make a permanent shift to another central communication form. Although members will experience conflicts within this cohesive group, the stability of a central communication form helps regulate the intensity of their disagreements.

Although *lack* and *rigid* sound like absolute terms, they are relative in our usage. The degree of lack will vary from group to group, as will the degree of rigidity. Consistently healthy groups operate around a central but flexible communication form, instead of operating at one extreme or the other. (See the diagram.) Veering to either side of this balanced position, groups lose either the capacity to be centered or the capacity to be flexible. All groups at times, however, lose their equilibrium and become either less centered or less flexible, as every church leader knows.

EXTREME LACK OF CENTRAL COMMUNICATION FORM	CENTRAL AND FLEXIBLE COMMUNICATION FORM	EXTREME RIGIDITY OF COMMUNICATION FORM

Later I will discuss more specifically the various stages in which groups can be along this spectrum between the extreme lack of a central communication form and an extremely rigid communication form. The effort now is to describe those characteristics common to groups that lack a central communication form and to those that exhibit a rigid communication form.

Lack of a Central Communication Form

The search committee began its first meeting with pragmatic communication (where to meet, how often to meet, the time limits given them, the materials they would need). Some of the members anticipated that pragmatic communication would remain their modus operandi. Screening candidates, these members anticipated, would involve the step-by-step process of comparing each application with the given job description and required qualification. Pragmatic discussion of who was qualified and who was not would result in a slate of candidates to present to the consistory.

The first session ended with a vague understanding that the group's work was "selection based on criteria." Also vaguely present was the members' understanding that pragmatic communication would characterize their work together.

At the beginning of the second meeting, some members said that since the last session they had been rethinking the given job description. They wondered about the impact of this job description on the church's youth. They suggested that perhaps the required qualifications had originated more from looking at "successful churches" than from considering their own church's specific needs. In short, they moved decidedly to interpretative communication and away from pragmatic communication.

The group then became embroiled in interpretative communication. That form varied. Some members reinterpreted the job description and qualifications. Still others attempted to reinterpret the central nature of the group's task. Others began to make interpretations about the motives of those members intent on reinterpreting the church's job description or the group's given task. Occasionally a member issued a call to resume pragmatic communication. The meeting ended with members sensing that the group's agenda had been set back, or at least not advanced.

At the beginning of the third meeting, some members began to speak about how they were feeling (feeling communication). They talked about their previously undisclosed feelings regarding the gender of the associate minister, and about feeling uneasy with how things were going in the group. A few members tried to call the group back to pragmatic communication. One or two engaged in interpretative communication about what was happening in the group. The group, however, basically succumbed to feeling communication about male and female clergy and about personal experiences in the group.

In the fourth session, several individuals began to be critical of the committee chairperson and of other members siding with him (critical evaluative communication). He was accused of grandstanding, and his cohorts were accused of trying to impose their will on the group. Countercharges (critical evaluative communication) were hurled at the accusers. The meeting ended with people seriously upset with each other and doubtful about the group's chances for success. Some members then contacted the pastor asking for his help.

No doubt the personalities involved in the search committee contributed much to its lack of cohesion. The group's struggles might also be construed as a normal phase in the development of a new group. The functional difficulty of this group, however, was its lack of a consistent operational mode of communication. The group had been given a specific task by the church, but it had not been given a specific communication form with which to carry out that task. The absence of a clearly implicit or mandated communication form left them vulnerable to the "Tower of Babel" syndrome.

Well-functioning groups move fluidly between the various communication forms as the need arises. But without a central, organizing communication form, fluidity becomes fragmentation. The lack of a stabilizing communication form not only affects a group's ability to resolve conflicts, it creates conflict. In the vacuum of communication chaos, individuals become anxious, which either makes them defensive or leads them to try to impose order on others. Conflicts over control in groups often emerge from vulnerable egos, not just vaulting egos.

When a group lacks a central communication form, the ground is also fertile for what we might call the covert use of communication forms, in which an individual or subgroup uses a particular communication form for personal advantage. For instance, at the beginning of the fourth session, the chair of the search committee made an elaborate interpretation (interpretative communication) about how devastating the group's disharmony would be on the whole church body if it continued. He spoke of how the group had been entrusted with the future of the church, and that conflict in the search committee would have a lasting impact on the spirit of the congregation and the work of the new associate. The issue here is not the insightfulness of the interpretation but its function. His interpretative communication was used for a covert purpose, namely, as it was later revealed, to protect his reputation as a leader. His aim of avoiding criticism and garnering praise was concealed but carried out through a presumably good-faith interpretation (interpretative communication).

Following this interpretative barrage, the chair then switched to pragmatic communication. He made a formal proposal that a unanimous vote be mandatory for acceptance of any candidate. This, he said, would result in a final group consensus and would bode well for the new associate and the congregation as a whole. Since he and his cohorts com-

prised a majority vote, the resolution passed. Here pragmatic communication (around the issue of voting procedures) was also used for covert
reasons, in this case to coerce different-minded members into compliance and to preserve the chair's reputation. Recalcitrant members would
now feel guilty for holding things up or for being the ones who made the
group fail. As one member said concerning the chair, "With that plan
he'll come off looking good, and we'll be the bad guys."

The covert use of feeling communication was evident as two members claimed that they were so hurt that they would have to quit the
group unless things changed. They may certainly have experienced pain,
but their feeling communication served the surreptitious purpose of
manipulating the group.

Covert use of feeling communication is a growing problem. A
group's ability to communicate about a person's pain is typically minimal. The sensitivities of an injured party disturb the group, especially
when the party claims special rights and entitlements as a result of the
injury. As a result, the group tends to look for quick fixes that will dispel
the disquieting feeling communication. In groups, therefore, power often
swings to the dependent, the weak, the victim, who may use feeling communication for personal advantage. The danger of disgruntled individuals in groups is not so much their contrary opinions. The danger occurs
when they wed their contrary position with the fervor of victimhood.

The presence of a central communication form helps keep the group
honest, in a sense. It helps defend against the invasion of human frailties
in the form of selfishness, denial, and blaming. The group as a whole,
plus individual members, tend to be deterred from covert use of communication forms when a central communication form organizes its
labors and defines its identity.

A congregation as a whole can lack a central communication form.
The congregation may have structure and a program, but little cohesion.
"People do their own thing," lamented one pastor. "There is no organization or person through which things are cleared. Groups operate just
as independently as individuals. No discussion or coordination happens.

It's like everyone thinks the church is theirs to do with as they want." As the pastor and I worked together, we realized that the church had no community voice, no central communication form that helped weld them together as a cooperative unit with a corporate identity. Everyone spoke his or her own language.

Understanding this helped the pastor understand why his sermons were regularly criticized, but by different persons. Even when he varied the central communication form he used in the pulpit, it never failed to elicit dissatisfaction from someone, because the congregation lacked a major voice (a central communication form) that he could regularly join. His frustration at not knowing how to communicate with this congregation stemmed in large part from being in a congregation that lacked a consistent and reliable communicative core.

Rigidity of a Central Communication Form

The converse of an absent central communication form is a rigid central communication form. The term *rigid* is not used here in a moral sense but in a descriptive sense to suggest that group boundaries have been established and group practices initiated around an isolated communication form that restricts the operations of the group.

Rigidity of a central communication form may be temporary. For example, a church council became panicky when its senior pastor left. They immediately riveted themselves together around frenetic pragmatic communication. Discussing emergency arrangements consumed them. The most devastating consequence of this communication rigidity was to dictate to the church staff members the new tasks they would need to assume in the absence of the senior minister, without any prior consultation with the staff.

The group's rigid pragmatic communication ruled out the option of feeling communication, in which members might have expressed their own anxieties or resonated with the anxieties of the staff. It limited interpretative communication, in which they might have asked if the new tasks were appropriate for the staff to assume, or what meaning these new tasks might have for the personal identity of staff members. It curtailed evaluative communication, in which affirmation of the church's strengths or its abiding values may have given reassurance to everyone. This council was not bad, but rather temporarily impaired as its members momentarily congealed around a rigid communication form.

Rigidity of a central communication form sometimes may be habitual. A finance committee began to make plans for a church rummage sale. The members' pragmatic communication orientation lead them, from the start, to ask arrangement questions: when, where, who. That habitual communication form, however, disinclined them from spending time in interpretative communication, where meaningful questions needed to be raised first, such as the appropriateness of this type of project and the significance of having to depend on such fund-raising projects to keep the church afloat. Many pastors know the frustration of groups that habitually plan without serious reflection.

The rigid feeling communication of the Bible study group cited earlier also arose habitually. The group did not plan to organize itself in this narrow way. But once begun, it perpetuated itself. Sharing of intimacies and exposure of inner feelings became the ticket of admission for acceptance.

Rigidity of a central communication form also may be assumed as proper. A pastoral relations committee assumed that its proper role was "to help the pastor understand the nature of the church and the effects of his ministerial behavior." Acting somewhat like a pastoral counselor who would offer only interpretations to parishioners, this committee related only through interpretative communication. The pastor's analogy was different: "I feel they're like bosses who are constantly evaluating my performance. I don't feel treated as a person."

As a result of its rigid interpretative communication, the committee failed to engage in feeling communication, where the pastor might sense being treated as a human being rather than as a paid professional, and where he could take the group's feeling communication as an invitation to express his own feelings. Diminished also was evaluative communication, wherein the pastor and committee could offer mutual affirmations and work through grievances. Even pragmatic communication was minimized, shutting off the possibility of the minister feeling in partnership with the committee in solving parish problems.

In some cases, rigid interpretative communication of a group appears very similar to the rigid evaluative communication of a group. For instance, in a worship committee steeped in interpretative communication, new ideas for the church services were considered first and foremost in the light of a particular theological interpretation regarding worship. In quick order, consequently, the group interpreted that inclusive language in worship was contrary to biblical terminology and church tradition. Regimented around interpretative communication, this committee failed to shift creatively to other communication forms. Without feeling communication, the committee rendered itself immune to other people's yearning for expanded religious experiences and to the pain engendered by restricted religious language. Without pragmatic communication, the committee failed to examine if its interpretative decisions were working. Without evaluative communication, the committee failed to judge its own deliberations. Groups can suffocate relationships by cutting off the breath of broad communication.

Rigidity of a central communication form may be a declared stance. A programming group in the church made clear that it operated exclusively from evaluative communication. Every proposed activity was judged by a strict code of right and wrong. A suggestion for an AIDS seminar was summarily dismissed without discussion. The possibility of a pulpit exchange with a neighboring minister known for her liberal views was nixed. Movies to be shown to groups in the church were appraised as either "of God" or "of the Devil." These restricting acts were fueled by more than just a rigid communication form, of course. The quality of the group's communication, however, reinforced and re-created the emotional-cognitive climate of the group. As we have noted, communication forms both reflect and perpetuate group process.

Just as a congregation as a whole can lack a central communication form, a congregation as a whole can manifest a rigid communication form. One parish that considered itself made up of self-starters perpetually immersed itself in pragmatic communication. Conversation focused on projects to do, arrangements to be made, schedules to be followed. Individuals who came to the church needing to explore the meaning of life and the meaning of the gospel (interpretative communication) felt out of place. Other individuals seeking emotional support and the opportunity to share their experiences (feeling communication) felt isolated.

When a communication form is rigidly used, the other communication forms are severely compromised or are ruled as out of order. What often appears as the black-and-white thinking of a group often reflects the single-mindedness of a single communication form. That communication form structures the reality of the group, but in a narrow way. Access to new ideas and new ways of communicating is limited. The group gives formulaic solutions to problems and makes unqualified generalizations.

When a group operates from a rigid central communication form, it also tends to speak for each individual rather than the individual speaking for himself or herself. The group members act as if they know what everyone else is thinking, feeling, valuing, or planning. A kind of group tribalism arises, a homogeneity that gives cohesion but with inflexible boundaries. Interchanges with others groups, consequently, are restricted. Sentences may pass between groups but no real listening and no real understanding occur. In severe cases, communication rigidity perpetuates categorical representation, in which the group declares that its interests can be understood and articulated only by those who "speak our language."

The more intentionally a group holds on to its particular communication form, the more rigid that group is, and the more difficult it will be for the pastor to guide it toward communicative alternatives.

APPROACHES FOR CAREGIVERS

The previous thoughts can be summarized in two sentences. First, church groups may experience one of two basic types of communication problems: lack of a central communication form or rigidity of a central communication form. Second, these communication problems vary in intensity, which must now be discussed in order to identify realistic approaches for church leaders.

Earlier I diagrammed the general spectrum between "extreme lack of a central communication form" and "extreme rigidity of central communication form," with "central and flexible communication form" as the healthy center. I said that later we would spell out the stages that groups can be in along this spectrum.

My work with struggling groups finds them somewhere at or between three stages to the right or left of center. The following diagram shows the three stages of groups marked by a rigid central communication form.

CENTRAL AND FLEXIBLE COMMUNICATION FORM	Stage 1	Stage 2	Stage 3	EXTREME RIGIDITY OF COMMUNICATION FORM

Stage 1 can be called "transitory." In this stage, rigidity of communication is temporary. This happens commonly with groups going through change or experiencing acute anxiety. The church council that panicked and did not consult the church staff is an example of a stage 1 group. Such groups are the most eager to accept help with their communication problems.

Stage 2 can be called "habitual." Here the rigid communication form is assumed to be proper or has become routine. The financial committee and the Bible study groups referred to in the last section exemplify groups in this stage. The pastoral relationships committee and the worship committee are more intense examples of the stage 2 group.

In the habitual stage, groups are still capable of learning new communication skills, though their communication patterns are harder to change than those of stage 1 groups. Familiarity and routine also tend to lead all groups back to old communication habits, even when new patterns have been learned.

Stage 3 can be called "institutionalized." Here the rigid communication form has been declared as the authorized way for the group to relate to the world. It has been reinforced by church ritual and group approval, and it is part of the group's conscious identity and practice. The programming committee discussed above and the church of "self-starters" are two examples of stage 3 groups. Groups at this stage are difficult to change.

The approach I suggest for rigid communication groups is most productively used with stage 1 groups. It can also be used fairly effectively with groups in the early phase of stage 2. By itself, however, this approach will not be sufficient for dealing with communication problems of groups who are solidly in stage 2 and stage 3 and will need to be supplemented by other approaches. *This communication approach, however, will be the basis for dealing with all groups, no matter how rigid their communication form.*

The same stages exist on the spectrum from "central and flexible communication form" to "extreme lack of central communication form."

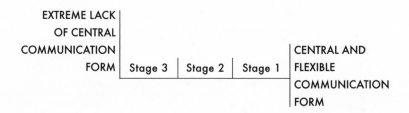

In this diagram, stage 1 also represents "transitory" communication problems of groups lacking a central form, and stage 2 represents "habitual" communication problems of groups lacking a central form. Stage 3, however, is best labeled "characterological" rather than "institutionalized" communication problems. In such groups there are no ritualistic acts validating the lack of communication cohesion as part of the group's identity. And yet such communication anomalies appear to be indigenous to the character of these groups.

The approach I suggest for dealing with groups lacking a central communication form is most productive for groups in stage 1 and the early phases of stage 2. Although this approach will need to be supplemented by other approaches for groups solidly in stages 2 and 3, *it will be the foundation for all work with all groups no matter what their severity.*

My primary effort in working with groups is to guide them so that they can function on task, that is, fulfill their given mission, whether that be service, mutual care, or administration. In attempting to do that, I basically approach groups from two levels of communication: pragmatic and evaluative. From the stance of pragmatic communication I attempt to direct groups. From the stance of evaluative communication I attempt to encourage them. The following discussion highlights how pastors can use directing and encouraging to help groups with their communication problems.

Using Pragmatic Communication to Direct Centralized Communication

In general terms, directing is advisable at the beginning of a group's life together, where a central communication form appropriate for the group's operational life should be clearly identified. Directing is also necessary when a group's mandated task is in jeopardy due to the lack of a central communication form.

In an effort to develop communication cohesion, I give groups four directives. *(1) Communication must remain open among members.* This helps to overcome isolation of members and the splitting off of members into subgroups. *(2) The group should be the primary arena for communication.* This helps to overcome the tendency of members to go outside the group to communicate about problems or to seek solutions. *(3) The group should focus its work around a specific central communication form.* At times an appropriate communication form will be specified to the group as part of its identity and pattern of work. At other times the pastor will help a group find its own appropriate central communication form. *(4) The group should monitor its disagreements.* Disagreements should reflect members' efforts to productively embody the central communication form, rather than reflect disagreement with the central communication form or covert use of communication forms.

I try to incorporate these four directives artfully in specific situations. The following case illustrates how the minister confronted by members of the search committee sought to be directive.

The minister began by listening carefully to those members who came to him. He not only heard their report that "our communication fell apart," he also took seriously this interpretative appraisal of their difficulty. In addition, he hypothesized that the divergent communication approaches of members and the competition between them represented the lack of a central communication form. That hypothesis was strengthened by the realization that the group had not been given an appropriate communication form to use in its work as a search committee.

Working on the premise that the group's disorder stemmed from communication problems, the pastor was prepared to deal with the group's communication. After expressing concern for those members visiting him (feeling communication) and offering appreciation for their efforts (affirming evaluative communication), he took a pragmatic communication approach in which he gave these directions: "Go back to your group. Tell them you have asked for my help. I will contact the chairperson to let him know that I will be visiting the group soon with some pertinent information you need."

In this simple pragmatic directive the pastor aimed to accomplish a number of things that would aid the group's communication and cohesion. First, he steered the members back to the group. Although they had a right to come to him for help, he indicated that they were still part of the group, and that the primary communication should occur in the group. This expressed the directive that communication should be group contained.

Second, he directed them to maintain open communication. He told them to tell the group that they had been to see him. Secret alliances or unexpressed maneuverings undercut group cohesion and the development of a workable central communication form.

Third, and most importantly, the pastor set the stage for doing what should have been done from the outset: establishing a central communication form for the search committee. In this situation, that central form mostly likely would have been pragmatic communication.

The pastor met the search committee as a whole at its sixth meeting. He began by thanking the members for their commitment of time and energy (affirming evaluative communication), and he expressed concern for the struggles they were going through (feeling communication). He then went on:

> As you know, several members of this group came to me. They were concerned about the difficulty you have been having communicating with each other. I told them to share with you that they had been to see me. It is important in any group for members to establish open lines of communication with each other. Without members being open with each other, cooperation and mutual respect never have a chance to develop.
>
> You need to be open with each other. I will be open with you. Any information you give me about the group, please be pre-

pared to give also to the group, for I will consider it the
property of the group and handle it accordingly.

That connects with something else. For groups to develop a
working atmosphere, their communication must be group
contained. That means that the basic place where your communication about your work should occur is in the group,
not outside the group. The chairperson will normally report
your progress to the church council from time to time, of
course, but your communication as a group should stay in
the group.

I will do the same. Our conversation here tonight is part of your
ongoing work as a group. I will not be sharing it with anyone else.

To this point, the pastor had given two of the four directives. He
tried to do it in a sensitive but straightforward manner, amplifying the
directives with brief explanations (interpretative communication). He
also laid the directives upon himself as well as upon the group as a way
to indicate that the directives were not dictatorial but pragmatically necessary for productive group communication.

He then continued: "In your work you are being hampered by not
having data you should have had from the start. You were assigned a
task, but you were not assigned a central communication form to use
and be organized around. It is now my responsibility to give you that
information."

The pastor then briefly described the nature of pragmatic, feeling,
interpretative, and evaluative communication. He explained how successful groups are organized around one central communication form,
even though they use the other forms flexibly as the need arises. He then
gave the third directive: "Your basic communication in this committee is
to be pragmatic in nature. You have a list of the qualifications the church
is looking for. You have reports from candidates who are telling us about
their qualifications. Your task is to match the reports to the list of quali-

fications and see who may be viable candidates. Your communication should deal with the pragmatic issues of this screening process."

In an effort to clarify the centrality of pragmatic communication, he differentiated it from other communication forms:

> If the central communication form of this search committee were to be interpretative communication, the council's directive to you might have been: "Your basic communication in this group is to be interpretative in nature. You are to converse about the possible meanings and implications of the criteria we have proposed for the life of this congregation. Your communication, therefore, should be of an reflective quality."
>
> If the central form of this search committee were to be feeling communication, the council's directive to you might have been: "Your basic communication in this group is to be feeling in nature. We are relying upon your felt reactions to the various candidates, how they strike you, what impressions they make upon you. Sharing feelings with other members of the group will also be part of your communication work together."
>
> Finally, if the central form of a search committee were to be evaluative communication, the council's directive to you might have been: "Your basic communication in this group is to be evaluative in nature. You are to judge which candidate most embodies the theology of this church and the presence of the Holy Spirit. Your conversation, therefore, should be focused on deciding which candidate measures up to our religious standards."

Like this search committee, groups are typically given tasks to accomplish but no directives on how to communicate. They are given a name and a description for their task but are not given guidance on how they could best talk together. As we have indicated, groups that lack a central communication form fail to achieve cohesion and productivity. Part of our pastoral responsibility is to help each group stay focused by maintaining a central communication form appropriate to its nature. In many cases pastors will need to be directive in order to give the group a voice. At other times we will need to help a group find its own voice. The establishment of a central and appropriate communication form, however, is the main goal.

A member of the search committee responded to the pastor: "But some of us think the congregation needs a different kind of associate than the criteria lays out." The pastor replied: "That type of conversation would be very appropriate in another group, but it does not apply here. Pragmatic communication around this screening process is your assigned role. Not just the task but the central communication form is what draws you together as a working committee."

Another member then spoke up: "I don't think I can continue. This is not what I had in mind when I joined this group." It was then that the pastor incorporated the fourth directive:

> Because you did not have all the information you were entitled to have at the beginning, any one of you who wishes to withdraw from this group can do so with your respect in tact and with our deep appreciation for your efforts to this point. But everyone who stays with the group is called upon to participate in pragmatic communication as the dominant form in which this group carries out its work.
>
> Disagreements between you, if they arise, should be monitored. Those disagreements should reflect your best efforts to communicate pragmatically about the screening process before you. Those disagreements should not be disagreements with the task, or with the central communication form, or with each other personally.

Once again, this also applies to me. In my work with you, I will approach everything from the perspective of pragmatic communication. Even if there are future snags in your work, I will consider them in terms of your central communication form, pragmatic communication, and try to help accordingly

These four steps provides a strategy for pastors. They can be used with all groups at all stages along the spectrum from central and flexible communication form to extreme lack of a central communication form. I will not attempt to discuss here how other auxiliary approaches must supplement work with groups solidly at stages 2 and 3. Prevention and immediate repair of communication problems are often the most important ministerial acts in any case.

Using Evaluative Communication to Encourage Centralized Communication

To help groups become cohesive through the development of a central communication form, I also communicate from the evaluative mode, particularly in the form of encouragement. Encouragement is an essential ingredient for a good life and for a productive group. We can become our best self only through the encouraging voice of others. Groups, likewise, function best when they feel affirmed.

While pastors seem routinely to encourage groups, our encouragement is often used as a "shot in the arm" rather than as a constant resource for growth. Furthermore, our encouragement is often made a parting gesture, a closing benediction, rather than a tool for change. While encouragement needs to be heartfelt, it also needs to be understood and wisely applied.

The pastor offered to the search committee what we can call effort encouragement. As noted above, he praised the efforts of those who came to him for help, praised the efforts of the search committee when he met the members at the sixth session, and praised the efforts of those members who might withdraw. *Affirming evaluative communication regarding the efforts of groups and their members creates a supportive climate for the practice of open communication, group-contained communication, use of a central communication form, and monitoring of communication disagreements.*

Besides effort encouragement, we can minister to groups with competence encouragement. In another setting, the pastor and church council openly affirmed the group for its ability and for its knowledge put into practice.

Finally, clergy can offer image encouragement. This involves, on the one hand, holding before the group pictures of what it *can become.* "You are a better group than you think you are," said the pastor to the search committee, "and you can do more than you think you can." Groups grow toward the images they and others have about them. Visioning for a group how it can become more cohesive and more focused around a central communication form, for example, lures the members toward fulfillment of those visions.

On the other hand, image encouragement involves holding before the group pictures of what it is *called to be.* A communicated image about its calling helps forge a core identity and a commitment to the group task. One pastor expressed to a group that it was to be "God's healing balm," helping the church remain stable during a difficult time. Another pastor called a group "Christ's disciples," charged with bringing the story of the church to life. Affirming evaluative communication such as this is not manipulation of the group's actions but encouragement of its best efforts.

Using Pragmatic Communication to Direct Flexible Communication

Groups with a rigid communication form do not usually seek out the pastor for help with their communication. Those in stage 1 and the early part of stage 2 are receptive to pastoral guidance, however. In these cases, we clergy must not be fainthearted, for we will need to be directive in a decidedly hands-on way. We intervene as communication managers, attempting to free communication space and facilitate new communication in which unexplored options can be discovered.

The four directives for groups experiencing rigidity of a central communication form are just the opposite of those for groups lacking a central communication form.

1. Block communication (rather than keeping communication open).
2. Encourage communication outside the group (rather than keeping communication contained within the group).
3. Encourage alternate communication forms (rather than focusing around a central form).
4. Monitor the lack of disagreement (rather than monitoring disagreements).

When a group is enmeshed in one particular communication form, that form needs to be blocked. Continued use of the communication form only reinforces its hold. Blocking helps release group members from the dominating form so that different forms of communication can arise. Blocking at this point is more important than urging open communication, for the latter may do nothing but perpetuate the status quo. Members may communicate more openly around the very form that restricts them, but such openness is counterproductive.

On the one hand, therefore, I may direct a group to cease and desist. I might have said to the emergency-minded council, "Your pragmatic communication about how to handle matters was a good thing, but it has become too much. Whether you know it or not, it has become so intense that it has restricted other approaches to the problem. So, you need to put a lid on it for a while. This group needs to take a break from further pragmatic communication with each other."

On the other hand, I may also direct the group to communicate through the pastor, instead of internally. In order to break up especially rigid communication, I become the gatekeeper of communication by having all communication channeled through me. I may say: "For the time being, direct your conversations to me. Even if you are responding to what someone said, say it to me rather than directly to the person. That way I can help you talk to each other in some different ways." That may sound like a foreign idea to pastors. It certainly has the pastor asserting himself or herself. Care of souls, however, necessitates doing what is necessary.

The second major directive is for group members to get out and mingle. A rigid communicative form creates group members who insulate themselves from other persons with different ways of communicating. Group-contained communication in this situation is detrimental. I direct members to speak to others outside the group, to hear new ideas, to get different opinions they can bring back to the group: "Talking about the work of this group to outsiders is not to be disloyal. If anything it shows a healthy respect for this group, because you are doing all you can to help the group do its work in the best manner possible."

The third directive is to alternate communication forms. This can be structured into the group's process in one of two ways. One way is by directing the establishment of communication subgroups that will act as peer consultants to the group. Each form of communication is to be represented by at least two members of the group, who volunteer or are appointed. In the group, and sometimes at special meetings outside the group, I instruct these subgroups in the type of communication they are assigned to represent. My general directive to the group as a whole is this: "Whatever task or issue may arise, approach it from all four communication modes. Let your subgroup leaders lead the discussion from each of the four modes." In this version, advocates for each communication form are established, and the use of alternative forms is structured into the group's process. The goal is the full utilization of all communication forms.

A rigid communication group will experience consternation when first working with this new communication framework. For a while the group may even be less productive than before, but these disturbances will lessen. A dominant form of communication will normally appear—

maybe even the form around which the group was rigidly formed—but now the other communication modes will more than likely have their due influence on the group.

A second way to structure use of alternative communication forms is to direct the establishment of a communication observer, a more low-keyed procedure for helping the group vary its communication. A member from the group is designated as a participant observer whose task is to reflect to the group the nature of its communication. The communication observer, unlike the communication subgroups, is not required to initiate communication changes. The group in this version, unlike the group that is required to communicate diversely, is left with the responsibility to alter its own communication once it is made aware of its problems by the observer.

The degree of communication rigidity and the nature of group members determine which method to use. In each case, pastors should try to install a structure that will consistently aid the group's communication and thus the quality of its life together.

The final directive to the group is for members to monitor their lack of disagreement. A group with a central and flexible communication form has normal differences of opinion, along with different perspectives from the different communication forms. The absence of disagreements, alternative suggestions, or creative friction is likely to indicate that the rigid communication form has returned. I would advise the group to "pay attention to the lack of disagreement between you. Be suspicious when a kind of group-mindedness sets in. That may not be the sign of a group functioning together smoothly, but of a group playing only a single note."

Using Evaluative Communication to Encourage Flexible Communication

A group marked by a rigid communication format is fragmented from others. Its mind-set results in separateness and in alienation from important understandings and feelings. Critical evaluative communication from the pastor in the form of chastising may jolt the group, but it militates, in the long run, against creative adaptation.

Pastors, however, do need to confront the actions of rigidly communicating groups. One way to do this while still remaining supportive is to encourage discontent with the status quo. Without a substantive degree of discontent with how things are, groups and their communication forms remain the same. Ask the group, "Are you really satisfied with how this group communicates? Do you really believe in your heart that your way of communicating with each other nurtures the best in you and the best in others? Aren't there times when how you talk begins to sound stale, mechanical, lifeless?" Along with this encouragement of discontent, the pastor at some point may begin to rally a few members who will initiate a change in the group. That was the underlying intention in establishing communication subgroups or a communication observer.

With rigidly communicating groups I also encourage virtuous communication. Communication in groups is not about the right to communicate, but about the right *way* to communicate. Communication has to do with character, with virtue. Rigid groups hold on tightly to their declared right to communicate. Healthy groups espouse virtue and strive for the right way to communicate. "Good character comes from communicating virtuously in groups," I may say to a group, "and by being in groups where virtuous communication is encouraged and rewarded. Without virtuous communication, a group cannot function well. It cannot be all it was called to be."

Working with groups and their communication can be rewarding for clergy. It is often long and delicate labor, however. We must monitor ourselves lest we fall into critical evaluative communication when groups resist the communication changes we know would benefit them and the church. Communication problems are not simply headaches that interfere with our ministry. They are the very problems we have been called to heal through our ministry.

everend James listened carefully as Mrs. Samsa, a woman from his congregation, once again summed up her distress: "So, I've always tried to be helpful to my daughters, my husband, my friends, and our neighbors. I give them advice from my own experience to help them out. But what do I get for that? No appreciation. The more I try to help them, the less thanks I get. My feelings are hurt. I feel used by them after all the guidance I've offered."

"It does hurt when our good intentions are not received as we expect," responded Reverend James. "Let me ask a question about what you've shared. It's a question that seeks to understand what is happening rather than to be critical. I wonder if you were trying to use your advice as a way to show how you felt about them?"

"Well, of course," replied Mrs. Samsa. "My giving advice is showing how much I care for them. That should be obvious."

"I understand that, especially since we're talking about your feelings," reflected Reverend James. "Unfortunately, it may not be obvious to others. Maybe people are unaware that your pragmatic communication is suppose to express your feelings about them. Maybe all they hear is the pragmatic advice but not your concern."

We experience our words as part of our very self. They are emanations from our mind, embodiments of our personality, the extensions of our body intended to shape the world around us. Our words are not only personal, but also creative. How we communicate structures both our experiences and our relationships. Our communication constitutes our reality and is not merely commentary on it.

This understanding of the personal-creative dimension of our communication is especially important as in the next chapters we discuss two significant communication problems of individuals, beginning first with substitution. Here individuals routinely use one communication form as a substitute for another. This problem is familiar to pastors but not usually identified. As pastors become aware of the different forms of substitution I discuss below, other manifestations will likely come to mind. By helping individuals address this problem, we not only help them work through their difficulties, but we also help prevent difficulties. Communication problems accumulate and proliferate. Dealing with them early mitigates against their power to corrode lives.

Substitution is not based on a simple misunderstanding of terms. A substitution is a lived habit, part of an individual's orientation, of what seems normal. An individual may speak as if one communication form were embodied in another, may assume that two forms are functionally equivalent, or may believe that one form can represent another. The problem here is not that one form carries too much communication freight. The problem is that one form is not carrying the expected communication freight at all, or is carrying freight the communicator did not expect. The result is personal and relational distress.

Basic to Mrs. Samsa's problem was *acting as if pragmatic communication were feeling communication.* For her, giving advice (pragmatic communication) was a way to show her feelings (feeling communication). Unfortunately, others did not perceive that. Recipients of her advice heard no feeling communication. They heard only advice. She seemed to expect others to acknowledge and follow her directives. As a result, there appeared to be no opening to engage her on the feeling level. She was the counselor; they were the client. Eventually that relationship wore thin, and people moved on to relationships marked more by explicit feeling communication. When that happened, Mrs. Samsa felt injured. Her "feelings were hurt," although she had not presented her feelings to others in identifiable ways. Her emotional concerns for others were not conveyed by the pragmatic communication she had substituted for feeling communication. The following substitutions also commonly occur.

The man who suggested to his wife that they simply write down all their disagreements and then pragmatically resolve them substituted *pragmatic communication for interpretative communication.* Not only did he rush in to try to fix the relationship before he understood it, his very pragmatic approach served as his explanation of the relationship. When his frustrated wife tried to explain (interpretative communication) that there was more meaning to the problems between them than simply pragmatic snags, he countered with the comment, "If the problem is resolved the way I'm suggesting, isn't that an indication that was the problem in the first place?" Substituting pragmatic communication for interpretative communication leads individuals, like this man, to think that knowing how to handle a situation is equivalent to knowing the meaning of the situation. Such is not the case.

Pragmatic communication is sometimes substituted for evaluative communication. An old show tune says, "All I do I do for you." That evaluative statement can hearten a spouse, for example, because it is clearly a "for you" affirmation. But when "all I do" is expected to function as an unspoken affirmation, spouses lose heart. When Tevye in Fiddler on the Roof asks his wife of many years, "Do you love me?" she responds with a litany of all she does for him. He turns to her again with painful pleading, "But do you love me?"

Similarly, a husband stated, "I don't give compliments. When my wife says, 'How do I know you like the way I dress, or the way I make love?' I tell her to assume that everything is all right unless I tell her that changes are necessary." Here, too, pragmatic communication functions in place of direct evaluative communication.

Feeling communication substituted for pragmatic communication is ubiquitous. For example, a spouse may assume that his or her expression of feeling will be sufficient to alter the partner's behavior. "Surely if I let her know how upset [sad, angry, etc.] I am, then she will change her ways," a husband might say. Feeling communication is expected to work out the problem. The spouse replaces explicit pragmatic communication with feeling communication assumed to serve the same function. At times the feeling level may be intentionally used as a means for eliciting changes, such as trying to induce guilt in persons or overwhelm them with emotions. But feeling communication substituted for pragmatic communication often occurs without explicit planning.

Many people have never really communicated pragmatically. They have always operated through their feelings and have felt defeated when feeling communication has not solved problems. When they are introduced to other ways of dealing with difficulties, such as explicit pragmatic communication, they are often amazed. "I've never done this before," said one woman. "I simply come to everything through my emotions. When expressing my feelings has not worked, I've either talked louder or more dramatically." Talking louder or more dramatically tends to drive partners away. They tend to hear the feeling communication as uncontrolled emotions or frustrated complaints but not as pragmatic communication.

Individuals, as well as couples and groups, sometimes substitute *feeling communication for interpretative communication,* which may be the most pernicious substitution of all. In the most simple form, a person contends, "I know why it happened because I know how I feel." Expressing a feeling (feeling communication) is equated with giving/finding an explanation (interpretative communication).

For example, a parishioner who expressed being hurt by her pastor said, "I felt humiliated by what he did to me." That sounded like a simple enough statement, but as we talked about it more, it became clear that her feeling embodied her whole understanding of the situation. *"I felt humiliated* by what he did to me" (feeling communication) became *"he humiliated me"* (interpretative communication). She was saying, "I felt humiliated by what he did, therefore the reality is that he humiliated me." To *feel* humiliated meant to *be* humiliated. The humiliation came from somewhere outside herself; it was inflicted upon her. Furthermore, for her, feeling humiliated meant that the other person intended to humiliate her. Feeling communication became interpretative communication that named both perpetrator and motivation.

Those who are pointed to as the "cause" of such feelings are often nonplussed if not enraged. They have no opportunity to explain themselves because the "victim" has already articulated a conclusion (interpretative communication) based on expressed emotions (feeling communication). The person is saying, "I know how things are because I know what I feel." Acting as if feeling communication were interpretative communication leads ultimately to a lonely existence, for there is no perspective other than one's feeling perspective.

Substituting interpretative communication for pragmatic communication tends to be perpetuated by those of us in the helping professions, particularly those of us who are inclined to help individuals understand themselves and their situations. Interpretative communication can be very effective, as in the case of a friend of mine who tells of how renaming a crucial event in his life (interpretative communication) resulted in his being able to talk about new ways to manage that event (pragmatic communication). Some individuals, however, including mental health professionals, tend to shortcut the process and live as though interpretative communication were pragmatic communication. They assume that talking about the meaning of something is the same as dealing with it. "If I can just understand what is going on, then everything will be okay," said one woman.

Idealizing interpretative communication leads individuals to expect solutions from explanations. My wise friend, however, knew that renaming his alcoholism as a psychological disturbance rather than a personal failure (interpretative communication) was not equivalent to working on his alcoholism (pragmatic communication). The twelve-step program of Alcoholics Anonymous begins with interpretative communication (an explanation that those addicted are powerless) but moves swiftly to pragmatic communication discussing what one must do as a result of that explanation. Those who remain addicted often perpetuate their denial of alcoholism by making interpretative communication pragmatic communication. "I have a clearer idea what my problem is now," said one individual. "I don't need AA. I'll get along fine." For many alcoholic and other individuals, "talking the talk" (interpretative communication of a superficial nature) is substituted for "walking the walk" (pragmatic communication of a difficult nature).

Sometimes *interpretative communication is substituted for evaluative communication.* Interpretative communication is not value-neutral. It always contains elements of evaluative communication, although it is not a substitute for it. Some individuals, however, try to make it so. Their explanation of something (interpretative communication) is automatically taken as their assessment of something (evaluative communication). "Explanatory truth" becomes more than a value we all share; "explanation" becomes "the truth." A conceptualization of something (interpretative communication) becomes a value judgment regarding something.

An explanation about the stages of faith development (interpretive communication), for example, may be taken as what "ought" to happen (evaluative communication). In this case, defined developmental sequences are confused with value judgments. An explanation about church growth (interpretative communication) may be automatically accepted as a goal for all churches (evaluative communication). Here a description of a process becomes an ideal. An explanation about how pastors function may become expected aims whose fulfillment or unfulfillment determine the pastor's worth. The more vulnerable parishioners and pastors become, the more inclined they are to making interpretative communication evaluative communication.

A woman who lived with the motto, "To know me is to love me," used interpretative communication for evaluative communication. She expected that someone's understanding of her (interpretative communication) would mean their validating of her (evaluative communication). She had limited awareness that explaining herself did not spontaneously translate into being affirmed. Another individual believed that how well others conveyed understanding for his position (interpretative communication) indicated how well they regarded him. He, too, had difficulty experiencing that he could be understood but not affirmed, or not be understood but still affirmed. Relationships are distorted when interpretative communication functions as evaluative communication.

One of my personal failings is *substituting evaluative communication for pragmatic communication,* especially when my resources are low. For example, rather than talk to my children about resolving problems they are having or creating for others (pragmatic communication), I throw out a criticism (evaluative communication) that is suppose to alter their behavior: "Your room looks like a pigpen! When are you ever going to grow up and be responsible!" At that moment I'm substituting critical evaluative communication for pragmatic communication.

The same dynamic happens at times in my pastoral counseling. When I'm emotionally depleted, I may begin to utter empty words of praise to individuals coming for help. Rather than expend further energy on the hard work of pragmatic communication, I may use verbal strokes (affirming evaluative communication) to placate their worries. For example, I may say, "You're a good person. Things will work out for you." Or, "You're very likable. People will come around." This replacement for pragmatic communication is nothing more than a patronizing pat on the head. Invariably it erodes my self-esteem, along with the relationships I have tried to establish with those in need.

Preachers also sometimes substitute evaluative communication for pragmatic communication. Proclaiming how each person is a wretched sinner is expected to bring conversion. Preaching that one is deserving of hell (critical evaluative communication) is taken as preaching that releases one from hell (pragmatic communication). Conversely, proclamations that persons are created in the image of God and created good (affirming evaluative communication) are expected to motivate them and resolve their difficulties. Evaluative communication functions for pragmatic communication in ways that are not efficacious, or only temporarily so.

A sizable number of people live primarily from the evaluative level and *act as if their evaluative communication were interpretative communication.* Espousing one's values, standing up for what one deems right, naming what is bad and harmful (instances of evaluative communication) are essential expressions necessary for the wholeness of persons and society. However, throughout these pages we have seen how extremes of evaluative communication in the form of critical and affirming communication can be detrimental to human relationships. Announcing a moral injunction is not the same as interpreting a situation. Persons operating from a stance of moral pronouncements may not only fail to interpret the specific life situations of individuals, they may also act as if their pronouncements *were* the interpretation of individuals' life situations. But making a declaration that something is right or wrong, responding to a person or situation with a positive or negative moralistic judgment, is not interpretative communication.

"People who get AIDS deserve it," expounded one person in a manner that was clearly critical evaluative communication. That evaluative statement was all that he needed. The judgment represented the reality. The verdict was the understanding. "Abortionists are criminals," exclaimed another individual in the same manner. The moral sentence (critical evaluative communication) stood in place of moral understanding (interpretative communication). The quality of persons, the meaning of their acts, the moral dilemmas in which they found themselves did not need to be considered, for the sentence served as understanding.

On the other hand, blanket affirming evaluative communication is also not interpretative communication. To say, "He's all right. He's a (black, white, brown, etc.) brother," is to assume that validating one's color is understanding the person. Casting a benediction upon someone because of his or her race, nationality, gender, or economic status (affirming evaluative communication) is often taken as understanding who that someone is (interpretative communication). Intellectually individuals may know the difference between these two forms of communication, and yet they live as though evaluative communication were a sufficient substitute for interpretative communication.

APPROACHES FOR CAREGIVERS

Substitution is no minor problem, as individuals are often unaware that they are communicating in this way. They believe their communication patterns to be normal, and may not understand even when the substitution is pointed out. Mrs. Samsa may become disheartened when Reverend James tries to help her see that her pragmatic communication has not served as feeling communication. Another parishioner may respond with anger when a pastor suggests that his or her feeling communication is not interpretative communication.

Consequently, I try to stay flexible in my approach to this problem of substitution. Rather than counsel from only one stance, I select an approach that I think will bring a corrective communication experience but with the least threat to the individual's self-esteem. Below I highlight the general communication approaches we can take toward correcting substitution and offer some examples of what might be done in each.

Using Interpretative Communication: Reflecting

Pastors typically work from an interpretative communication stance. We try to broaden parishioners' understanding by making interpretations about them or others. We assume that their increased understanding will lead to new behavior, or at least to openness to new behavior. This is the basic approach Reverend James used in working with Mrs. Samsa. While he began with feeling communication (expressing empathy for her frustration), he moved decidedly into interpretative communication that sought to help her understand the nature of her problem.

He first asked an *interpretative question:* Was she trying to use her advice as a way to show how she felt about others? Interpretative questions do more than elicit data. They indicate the start of a reflective process in which parishioners are invited to join. In order to minimize the possibility of his interpretative question being take for critical evaluative communication, Reverend James also clearly stated his intention to seek understanding rather than to be critical. In doing so, he helped to establish a working relationship based on interpretative communication.

From listening to Mrs. Samsa, Reverend James suspected that she engaged in substitutions other than pragmatic for feeling. Her opening words suggested that she substituted feeling communication for interpretative communication. Feeling unappreciated (feeling communication) was taken by her as the meaning of others' behavior (interpretative communication). Reverend James's interpretative question, however, rightly focused on just one substitution, namely the primary instance she brought to him. Reflecting on a single instance of substitution, rather than a general tendency for substitution, is preferable when beginning interpretative communication counseling.

Reverend James then continued with an *interpretative hypothesis:* Maybe other people did not perceive that her pragmatic communication was to be an expression of her feeling. He allowed time for Mrs. Samsa to think about that new interpretation and to express whatever feelings it aroused within her.

Beyond what our opening dialogue showed, Reverend James next gave considerable time to *interpretative amplification.* He explained to Mrs. Samsa the four levels of communication and discussed how difficulties can arise when one form is substituted for another. He gave examples of substitutions other than Mrs. Samsa's in order to help her grasp the general nature of this communication problem. In all these ways he tried to engage her in a reflective process where interpretations could broaden her understanding of her own communication difficulty.

It was only then that Reverend James moved to a pragmatic communication approach. He suggested to Mrs. Samsa the following solution: "So, as you might see, it would probably help if you explicitly communicated your concerned feelings for others rather than suppose that your pragmatic communication could serve that role." The changes Mrs. Samsa needed to make may have been apparent to her from the interpretative work Reverend James had introduced. Interpretative communication can lead to altered action. But Reverend James left nothing to chance. He suggested communication adjustments. In moving to pragmatic communication, he reinforced his interpretative communication efforts. The reflective process was solidified by the action process.

Using Pragmatic Communication: Acting

With the interpretative communication approach, we move basically from reflection to action. The pragmatic communication approach moves us basically from action to reflection. This latter approach is based on the following premise: If we can get a parishioner to undertake an action, then through the very performance of this action he or she may not only change but also be lead to new understandings. Prescribing a new communication action, therefore, becomes a means for both altered communication and new reflections that sustain that altered communication.

If Reverend James had selected this approach, he would have first tried to engage Mrs. Samsa in performing a different type of communication. He might have said: "There is a way to communicate that may prove helpful to you. Perhaps you can try it. Every time you are moved to give advice as an expression of your concern for someone, simply tell them about your feelings for them instead. Try that for a week and let's see what happens." Although Reverend James would give brief interpretations (interpretative communication) about the purpose for this action, he would work with Mrs. Samsa primarily on the performance of her new communication. For example, he might rehearse with her what her general feelings might be and what she could actually say in expressing them to specific individuals. He might role-play with her about a particular encounter so she could practice not only what she would initially say but how she might respond to others' varied responses.

Reverend James might also suggest a distinct time frame for Mrs. Samsa's practice of feeling communication. He could indicate that they would meet after one week, for example, to see how her work had progressed. At that next meeting, Reverend James would ask how her practice had gone. If she had not tried to put feeling communication into practice, Reverend James could once again prescribe feeling communication, especially in those circumstances where she was inclined to give advice (pragmatic communication) as a substitute for feeling communication. If she had practiced as instructed, he could talk with Mrs. Samsa about what seemed to work and what didn't, and how she might make adjustments in her future efforts to convey feelings instead of give advice.

He could then ask Mrs. Samsa what she had experienced by using feeling communication. If she had gained awareness, Reverend James could move from pragmatic communication to interpretative communication. He could use her new experiences to help her reflect on the nature of her communication, specifically the issue of substitution. This could lead to discussion of how she had learned to substitute, how it had functioned in her life, and what personal meaning it might have for her. In doing this, Reverend James's pragmatic communication approach would be solidified by interpretative communication. Mrs. Samsa's altered communication would thus be reinforced—for the benefit of herself and others.

Using Feeling Communication: Emoting

Let's imagine that Reverend James approached Mrs. Samsa's substitution problem from the perspective of feeling communication. The primary focus then would not be on acting (pragmatic communication) or reflecting (interpretative communication) but on emoting (feeling communication).

In Mrs. Samsa's substitution of pragmatic for feeling communication, giving advice (pragmatic communication) functioned for expressing feelings (feeling communication). Her basic intention, however, was to convey feelings. That was the central intention of her communication. Reverend James's approach to this would be twofold. First, he would help Mrs. Samsa emotionally express her basic intention (expressing feelings). Deepening her emotional expression of this central intention would give it prominence and lay the groundwork for differentiating it from the substituted form of giving advice. He would then help her try to emotionally resonate with the feelings of others who received her advice. This felt sense of how others might experience her giving advice would also lay a foundation for discerning that a substituted form of communication would not be responded to in the same manner as her intended form of communication.

To help Mrs. Samsa emotionally express her own communication intention, Reverend James might say: "You feel hurt because your good advice has not been received as you hoped. Share again, from inside you, what you intended by giving advice." Here Mrs. Samsa would have an opportunity to express, and become more fully in touch with, her own deep and varied emotions about her intention to express her feelings for others. Reverend James would refrain from asking Mrs. Samsa to share more about her hurt feelings. The aim, instead, would be to enhance her emotional expression of the intentions behind giving advice. As Mrs. Samsa became increasingly expressive, Reverend James would affirm her emotions and the intent to which they pointed: "You express your feelings well, with great tenderness and compassion. That is what you want others to realize you feel about them when you give them advice." He would thus highlight again her concerned feelings as the central content she intended to have communicated by giving advice.

In using the feeling communication approach with other types of substitution problems, we can also focus on the basic intention of the individual's communication. In an interpretative-for-evaluative substitution, for example, the individual's basic intention is to communicate some assessment about a situation or person. The feeling communication approach emotionally highlights this basic affirming or disaffirming intention as a way of helping the individual differentiate it from interpretative communication.

Reverend James's next step would be to encourage Mrs. Samsa's emotional sensitivity to the reactions of others. He might say: "Now place yourself in the shoes of those for whom you have these feelings. You want them to know you care for them, with all the depth and richness you've just expressed. But can you imagine what they might feel if all they heard was the advice rather than your feeling? They might feel instructed rather than cared for. They might feel patronized rather than embraced. They might completely miss your intended feelings for them.

That could be a sad loss for all of you." This encouragement of her emotional resonance with others helps to disrupt the assumption that one form of communication is equivalent to another and carries the same message and impact.

Reverend James could then move toward an object lesson about substitution based on Mrs. Samsa's felt sense of the issue. He might say: "Your advice is not as expressive of your concerned feelings for others as directly sharing your feelings. You can sense that inside you. You can also sense that there is difference between the two."

A feeling communication approach to substitution can itself bring communication changes. Reverend James, however, could support this approach by moving next to more explicit interpretative communication about the forms of communication and the dynamic of substitution. He might say, for example: "Communicating advice is not same as communicating feeling. Sometimes, though, we try to let something else be a substitute for our feelings. Very often when that happens, it doesn't turn out for us the way we intended. That is probably what's happened with your communication." Finally, Reverend James could also move to more explicit pragmatic communication by discussing what communication adjustments Mrs. Samsa would need to make.

Using Evaluative Communication: Appraising

An evaluative communication approach would espouse some standard against which the individual's communication is appraised, such as Jesus as a model for life, or a biblical teaching, or an ethical principle, or a congregational norm. That standard would be expressed somewhere on the spectrum between critical evaluative communication and affirming evaluative communication. In general, a critical evaluative approach would focus on convincing the individual of his or her wrongdoing in communication and on the necessity of setting boundaries. An affirming evaluative approach would focus on convincing the individual of his or her goodness in communication and on the bolstering of self-esteem. There is no common standard against which substitution itself can be appraised, as substitution is not a recognized sin or self-limitation. But pastors may used general standards (from Jesus as model, or from biblical teachings, for example) and apply them to the particular problem of substitution.

If Reverend James had approach Mrs. Samsa from an affirming evaluative communication perspective using Jesus as the standard, he might have said: "Jesus calls us 'the light of the world.' We have the capacity to shine, for the good of each other and for the glory of God. When you substituted giving advice for expressing feelings, your light did not shine as well as it could. It kept you from being all you were called to be." Although Reverend James could then employ elements of the interpretative, feeling, and pragmatic approaches, this evaluative appraisal of Mrs. Samsa's communication, and her acceptance of it, would function as the prime motivation for change.

If Reverend James had approached Mrs. Samsa from a critical evaluative communication perspective with Jesus as the standard, he might have said: "Jesus warns us that 'It is not what goes into the mouth that defiles a person, but it is what comes out of the mouth that defiles.' Our words can be the occasion for harm to ourselves and others. That may be what has happened with your communication. Substituting advice for expression of feelings has created alienation. It is a problem to be seriously addressed." From here Reverend James may also utilize elements of the other approaches to help Mrs. Samsa set boundaries on her substitution problems.

The case we will discuss in the next chapter also involves pragmatic communication and feeling communication. This similarity will allow greater understanding of the differences between the communication problem of substitution and the communication problem of misalignment, to which we now turn.

T he phone rang just as Reverend Patel sat down for supper. It was a member of her congregation: "Lois is in the hospital. I've just left her in recovery. Doctors say cancer. The prognosis is bad. I've notified the insurance company. Now I've notified you."

Reverend Patel was stunned, both by the news as well as by Fred's businesslike tone. "I'm so sorry about Lois," she replied with genuine feeling. "I'll see her tomorrow morning. Right now, Fred, why don't I meet you at the hospital in an hour and we'll talk about it."

At times we can sense that what a parishioner is saying does not reflect what we imagine is happening inside him or her. Reverend Patel immediately recognized that Fred's words (form of communication) did not seem to fit the situation he was going through. In this chapter we look at a communication problem individuals basically have with themselves, that is, a problem of adequately expressing what is inside them. The problem is not one of substitution, where the person assumes that one form of expression is equivalent to another. The problem is one of misalignment, where one's form of communication fails to resonate with one's own inner experiences.

Pastors have been taught the importance of expressing what's inside oneself. We know that people stay healthy when their words resonate with their internal state of being and release what is there. Indeed, in our pastoral contacts we normally encourage individuals to express what is going on inside them and even help them choose words that are more in tune with their dominant state of mind at the moment. When words resonate with and release what is inside, we call this catharsis, an important step toward avoiding the build-up of internal tensions. We also recognize that verbalizing our inner experiences is necessary for facing these experiences and working through them. Finally, we also know that expressing to others what's inside us elicits their help in dealing with what is at the heart of our experience.

Much of our ministry in one form or another is directed toward helping individuals speak words that align with their inner experiences. When alignment happens, individuals' unknown, vague, or concealed experiences become acknowledged experiences. Their interior life becomes available as a resource for living.

In order to help parishioners communicate their inner experiences, we need a practical approach for thinking about an individual's dominant state of mind at any given time. I have found that the four forms of communication provide a basis for conceptualizing about our inner states.

When we listen to parishioners talk naturally, we sense that what they are saying expresses what is going on inside them, that their form of communication authentically represents their inner state of being. For instance, a person who interpretatively communicates about what it means to the church for the pastor to be ill is usually in an interpretative frame of mind. For this individual, inner experiences are focused around concerns for the meaning of something or the significance of an event, even though the specifics of that interpretative state may be varied.

An individual who pragmatically communicates about the best way to tell a child about the death of a pet is generally in a pragmatic frame of mind. For this person, experiences are oriented around decision making and problem solving.

People who complain about the noise before worship begins or compliment the pastor about the service (evaluative communication) tend to be in an evaluative frame of mind. The dominant experiences of individuals in an evaluative frame of mind center around judgments, appraisals, affirmations, or disaffirmations.

Finally, persons who speak of their embarrassment for calling someone by the wrong name or tell of sensing God's awesome presence (feeling communication) are commonly in a feeling frame of mind. It may be marked by anxiety, joy, grief, or some combination of emotions, but the person's state of mind at the moment is feeling-oriented.

As I try to understand the inner world of an individual, therefore, I find it helpful to think that there are four basic frames of mind corresponding to the four forms of communication we have been discussing. A person's dominant inner experiences at a given moment are embedded in either a pragmatic frame of mind, feeling frame of mind, interpretative frame of mind, or evaluative frame of mind. One's central frame of mind at any particular moment will contain dimensions of all frames, but one frame of mind will tend to be primary, just as one form of communication tends to be primary although dimensions of all four are present in each communicative act.

Expressed another way, at any given time dimensions of all four frames of mind are present, but one tends to be in the foreground while the others are in the background. From the perspective of our communication approach, an individual's primary frame of mind at a given time constitutes what is inside them. How an individual's form of communication fails to adequately communicate his or her frame of mind is the subject of this chapter, misalignment.

A person's frame of mind also has central content and a certain intensity. Communication misalignments occur when the structure, content, or intensity of a person's form of communication does not match the structure, content, or intensity of the person's frame of mind. As a result of misalignment, a person's internal experiences fail to be appropriately expressed and managed. For example, Reverend Patel may discover that Fred's external pragmatic communication about his wife is not aligned with his internal feeling state regarding her. Such a misalignment may be benign as an initial response but damaging as a continued response.

Structure misalignment, a first-order problem, occurs when two structures, the form of communication an individual is using and his or her frame of mind, are incongruous. Pastors encounter this type of communication misalignment most often in crisis situations.

For example, a woman stunned by the sudden loss of a loved one (feeling frame of mind) may speak exclusively from an interpretive form of communication about how all life must end and how everyone has a date with destiny. Then again, a grieving individual (feeling frame of mind) may communicate in an inappropriately pragmatic way. I remember, in this regard, a young woman who came for her counseling session and said, quite matter-of-factly, "My father died this week on the operating table. What else do you want to talk about?" Similarly, a man who was teeming with vile criticisms about another man who had insulted him (critical evaluative frame of mind) spoke about it in a measured pragmatic tone as if nothing significant had happened. This misalignment was not a judicious holding of one's tongue, which we all must do in certain situations; it was a deflection from his internal state that could ultimately cause him harm.

Reverend Patel sensed something of this communication misalignment with Fred. Fortunately such misaligned situations are often brief. Like Reverend Patel, we anticipate that after a while the person's form of communication will begin to match his or her frame of mind. Given time and encouragement, Fred will likely shift to feeling communication as an appropriate representation of his internal feeling framework.

Structure misalignments, however, may sometimes linger. I recall a seminary professor whose primary form of communication was affirming evaluative. In the weeks before he killed himself with a shotgun, he was full of praise for students and faculty. All the while, apparently, his frame of mind was pragmatic: dwelling on how to accomplish the central plan for his life—his death. The structure of his form of communication was severed from the structure of his frame of mind, with devastating results.

If an alignment does exist between the structures of form and frame, I then try to determine if *content misalignment* is the problem, if the content of the form of communication and the content of the frame of mind are incongruous. For example, Fred may turn to feeling communication and thus establish an alignment between his communication form and his primary mental frame, but the feelings he expresses (form content) may have little or nothing to do with his dominant internal feelings (frame content).

A misalignment between content of form and frame constitutes a second-order problem. We all know parishioners who talk about feelings other than the central feelings dominating their feeling frame of mind. We tend to be less worried about this situation than when the structure of their communication is severed from the structure of their frame of mind. We sense that these parishioners are at least going in the right direction (form and frame are aligned), and that eventually they will also travel on the right road (talk about central content).

Content misalignments, however, can be chronic. Pastors have heard the heartbreaking stories too often: the little boy who held the secret thought that he caused mom and dad's divorce; the little girl who did not tell about an uncle molesting her because she believed it was her fault; the woman who operated out of the assumption that she deserved to be abused; the man who harbored a false conviction that he was mentally inferior. Souls are damaged when the content of the form of communication and the content of the frame of mind are misaligned.

Finally, if I discern that an adequate alignment exists between content as well as structure, I then try to determine if the problem involves *intensity misalignment,* in which the intensity of the form of communication and the intensity of the frame of mind are incongruous. Fred may shift to a feeling form of communication that is aligned with his feeling frame of mind. In addition, the specific content of his form of communication may be aligned with the central content of his frame of mind. But the intensity of his form of communication may not be aligned with the intensity of his internal frame of mind. He may, for example, talk about his feelings concerning his wife's illness with a fervor that is either less or more pronounced than his inner frame of mind.

Misalignment between intensity of form and frame constitutes a third-order problem. Overall we tend to consider it the least dangerous and to assume that if individuals are traveling in the right direction (the structures of form and frame align) and are on the right road (the contents of form and frame align), then eventually they will travel at the right speed (the intensity of form and frame will align). Or, we may assume that the right speed is not all that important.

Speed, however, is dangerous. Misaligned intensity may cause problems. We know, for instance, that when grief is not expressed with the intensity with which it is experienced, it often surfaces in other ways. Likewise, when the intensity of an individual's critical evaluative communication is not aligned with the vehemency with which it is felt, it also may find debilitating outlets. Conversely, an intense profession of love (affirming evaluative communication) outstripping what the lover actually possesses may confuse the partner as well as prove disastrous for a relationship.

A wide range of personal and interpersonal difficulties can arise when misalignments distance an individual from his or her inner self. If Fred continued in his misalignment, he might distort what feelings he has, or lapse into a denial of his feelings, or his feelings may become disturbingly expressed in a variety of symptoms.

Once again we must lift up the important role of communication. On the one hand, an individual's internal state of being causes his or her communication to be misaligned. Fred may speak in a pragmatic form of communication because he is protecting himself from the pain of his feelings. Each of us can recall a time when we did not want to know what was going on deep inside us, or when we knew what was there but did not want to face it, or when we knew and faced it but did not want to share it with others. In these cases we misaligned our communication in order to avoid what was disturbing to us.

On the other hand, however, our communication misalignments cause us to remain distant from our inner experiences. When our external words do not resonate adequately with our inner life, we do not know what is going on deep within us, or we only vaguely know, or we cannot acknowledge what we do know. In pastoral conversations where form begins to match frame, parishioners will frequently say, "I didn't realize I was so filled with emotions" (feeling frame of mind), or "I'm surprised at how much I've thought about this" (interpretative frame of mind), or "I was unaware of how much of a decision I have already made" (pragmatic frame of mind), or "I've been more judgmental than I would like to acknowledge" (evaluative frame of mind).

Overcoming communication misalignments helps individuals overcome their resistances (the distancing of their form of communication from their frame of mind). It also helps individuals recognize what they implicitly know. Their frame of mind is brought to light through appropriate forms of communication.

APPROACHES FOR CAREGIVERS

Checking for communication misalignments can become part of clergy's regular practice and is especially important at the opening of a conversation with an individual, whether during a hospital call, home visit, or office appointment. Misalignments, however, may also arise later in the ongoing dialogue with a parishioner. Keeping our antennas out for this communication problem is part of our pastoral competency.

In order to consider some elementary ways to overcome misalignment problems, I suggest we operate from a combined feeling and interpretative communication orientation. Here we move back and forth between what we sense (feeling form of communication/frame of mind) and what we make of what we sense (interpretative form of communication/frame of mind). This feeling-interpretative orientation shapes our efforts to rectify structure, content, and intensity misalignments.

Using Feeling-Interpretative Communication to Empathize for Alignment

Dealing with communication misalignments of parishioners first requires communication with ourselves as pastors. Through a feeling-interpretative approach we pay close attention to how we are experiencing the individual and his or her form of communication. This involves three steps, which in much pastoral work are often done concurrently and partially. We can enhance our pastoral skill by deliberately focusing on these steps and following them in a sequential order.

The first step here, as in all pastoral relationships, is *empathic listening*. It means putting ourselves in a receptive, understanding mode as we try to absorb what a person, couple, or group is trying to communicate to us. We listen attentively to the specific story the individual is telling. We listen for who the characters are in the story, for the plot of the story as the person tells it, and for the story's defined difficulty. The question we ask ourselves here is, "What is the story the person communicates?"

The second step is *empathic sensing*, an attentiveness to the overall sensations created by the individual's communication. The question we ask ourselves here is, "How am I feeling about this communication in general?" Reverend Patel, for example, could ask herself, "Am I comfortable with the flow of what Fred is saying given what he has told me about Lois, or does something seem amiss? Do I detect a difference from how Fred usually talks?" Reverend Patel would pay attention to her empathic sense that Fred's communication was "off the mark," "too much," "not enough," or "atypical," for example.

If we sense that the form of communication seems natural and appropriate, then we might dismiss the possibility of communication misalignment and move on to other considerations. If we sense that the communication is peculiar in some way, however, we should continue our communication assessment.

The third step would then be *empathic imagining*. Here the question we pastors can ask is, "How would I communicate, or how would others typically communicate, if we were in this individual's situation?" Resonating with the individual's story and then looking inside at our own reactions, we empathetically imagine what a typical human response would be. From her own introspection, for example, Reverend Patel might say, "If I were in Fred's shoes, I'd probably talk about my feelings. I'd very likely say how worried I was for my spouse, or how scared I was for myself. And while I might not panic at this point, my expression of feelings would be more than just modest. I might shed a few tears or have a quiver in my voice. Something like that. That's also what I've come to experience with other people in similar situations."

Reverend Patel's empathic imagining would also include putting herself in Fred's shoes as a man, from a specific culture, several years older than she, who had perhaps been through unusual circumstances. Although she would try empathetically to understand Fred's unique reaction (why he is speaking so coolly about such an emotional issue), her first line of introspection would focus on the basic common response most of us humans would have, and which she hypothesizes by extension that Fred would have. This approach is based on the premise that individuals are more alike than different. Moreover, it honors the silent communication of individuals, namely those plans, emotions, thoughts, and judgments that often are not expressed through one's spoken communication.

By using empathic listening, sensing, and imagining, Reverend Patel could arrive at a working idea about the likely structure of Fred's frame of mind, of its possible content and intensity. She could then note whether the structure, content, and intensity of Fred's form of communication were generally aligned with what she assumed would be Fred's internal frame of mind. If a first-, second-, or third-order misalignment seemed to be present, then she could wonder if that signified communication problems with Fred or inadequacies in her own empathic efforts. She would recognize that no one's form of communication perfectly represents his or her frame of mind, and that no one's empathic efforts can perfectly envision the other's lived world. But in spite of these limitations, she could, on the basis of her empathic work, develop a plausible picture of Fred's frame of mind and the nature of his communication alignment.

Another way to assess an individual's dominant frame of mind using empathic imagining involves telling the individual's story from the perspective of each form/frame and then concluding which seems most likely as a common response. Reverend Patel, for instance, may rehearse the central events in Fred's current life situation from a pragmatic, feeling, interpretative, and evaluative perspective. From that she could draw a conclusion about which story told from which form and frame would seem most typical as a human reaction at that particular time.

This latter approach is particularly helpful when we have few clues about the person's lived situation. Reverend Patel has known Fred previously. She also knows that he has just received news about his wife, that it is bad, that he has been scurrying around making arrangements, that he has a need to call her, and that he seems to be communicating in a somewhat peculiar way. However, pastors often do not know that much about parishioners. We get bare outlines of stories. We get limited reactions. In those cases, we can use this method to tell parishioners' shadowed stories from each of the four frame perspectives and to hypothesize which frame of mind may be most dominant (and what the content and intensity of that frame might be). We can then begin to test our hypothesis through further dialogue with the person.

Regarding the professor I mentioned who committed suicide, I have often wished through the years that I had asked myself, "Is there another frame of mind dominating my beloved seminary professor other than what his form of communication suggests? What might it be, and where might it be leading him?" Imagining a different frame of mind for an individual may alert us to communication clues we have glossed over.

The pastor's effort to empathize for alignment is often done intuitively. Furthermore, we can sometimes quickly sense whether or not a person's form of communication embodies his or her inner story. In other cases we find ourselves giving extended time to empathic sensing and imagining. In all encounters with parishioners, however, we will need to continue being empathetically attuned to their communication, for only then can we more fully understand their frame of mind, their shifts in frame of mind, and the various ways forms of communication are aligned or misaligned.

In summary, our work to overcome communication misalignments begins by communicating with ourselves as pastors. Through the steps of empathic listening, sensing, and imagining we hypothesize about the structure, content, and intensity of an individual's current frame of mind that he or she may not be expressing adequately through his or her form of communication.

Using Feeling-Interpretative Communication to Facilitate Alignment

Some clergy are inclined simply to let individuals express themselves, which is appropriate when communication is functioning well. Facilitation is required, however, when communication problems exist. This does not mean that pastors have to become expert counselors. The communication approaches we have discussed for helping couples and groups can be implemented by any reasonably competent pastor. The same applies for aiding an individual's communication. The general principle is this: Our effort is to achieve first approximations, meaning that whether we are trying to facilitate alignment of structure, content, or intensity, *all we basically need to do is get individuals started.*

As I have figuratively said, in attempting to align the structures of form and frame we try to get the individual moving in the right direction. If Reverend Patel can get Fred to use feeling communication even sporadically, then that is adequate. In attempting to align content of form and frame we try to get the individual on the right road. Thus, if Reverend Patel can help Fred begin to address central feeling content even tangentially, that is adequate. Finally, in attempting to align intensity of form and frame we try to get the individual traveling at the right speed. If Reverend Patel can assist Fred to better communicate feeling intensity even marginally, that is adequate.

Once again, pastors do not have to function as pastoral psychotherapists who are trained to elicit a fuller expression of a person's frame of mind. Achieving first approximations is often enough to start a communicative process that will greatly benefit the individual. Experience shows that first approximations either make communication easier (the dam breaks, in a sense) or make communication more difficult (walls build up higher). If the latter happens, the pastor can strive again for first approximations. If repeated efforts fail, then a referral to a trained pastoral counselor or psychotherapist is advisable.

In order to facilitate structure alignment we must help an individual express his or her frame of mind. Stated more completely, we must stimulate the individual to begin to speak from a form of communication that is aligned with the structure of his or her primary frame of mind.

Toward this end, we pastors can use a series of approaches, beginning with some that are indirect and distant from the individual and ending with others that are personal and pointed. A pastor's first facilitating intervention can be launched from any one of these five levels. Sometimes the seriousness of a situation may require a more direct confrontation. Because people can be resistant, however, and tend not to be fully aware of their own dominant frame of mind, starting with the least intrusive levels may be most productive. This allows people to begin to speak more on their own and to feel more ownership of what they say. Although the following examples may seem abrupt and distinct, these approaches should be implemented smoothly during ongoing conversation with an individual.

As a start, we pastors can *communicate our own frame of mind.* Aware that her frame of mind was feeling-oriented when first hearing the news about Lois, and hypothesizing that Fred's frame of mind may be similar, Reverend Patel could use feeling communication and say: "I feel terrible about Lois. My heart aches for her, and for you, too, Fred." This approach demonstrates a particular frame of mind using our own expression of it and encourages a similar expression from individuals.

To further illustrate this step and others, let us consider the following pastoral contact. When visiting a man described by his worried family as very despondent, I found his communication to be strangely glib. After speaking with him for a while, I suspected that misalignment problems were involved. He was likely distancing himself from his frame of mind, or not adequately in touch with it. As I continued to listen to him talk, I empathetically imagined his frame of mind from each of the four perspectives. Based on that introspection and experiences with other depressed individuals, I decided to test out whether his dominant frame of mind was pragmatically oriented, particularly around suicidal thoughts and plans.

In an effort to facilitate expression of his supposed pragmatic frame of mind, I shared my own pragmatic frame of mind. I said, "As I listen to you, I keep thinking about the best way to be helpful to you. I keep trying to come up with a plan that will make things better for you." This verbalization of my own frame of mind attempted not only to express my emotional support but also to elicit communication about his own planning.

As a further effort to facilitate structure alignment, pastors can *communicate what frame of mind most people would probably be in* given a certain circumstance. Reverend Patel may say to Fred, "I suppose most people who hear about a loved one getting cancer are pretty shaken up." To the depressed individual I may say, "When most people are hurting inside, their first impulse is to find a quick solution, some way out." This approach normalizes a particular frame of mind and attempts to steer individuals toward recognition or articulation of their own similar frame of mind.

Switching to a more personal approach, we pastors can *ask the individual about his or her frame of mind.* In order to facilitate an expression of Fred's feeling frame of mind, Reverend Patel may ask, "How are you feeling, Fred? What are your feelings inside?" Similarly, I may ask the despondent man, "What thoughts have you had about how to deal with your grief?" in order to facilitate expression of his pragmatic frame of mind. Inquiries such as these prompt an individual to express a particular frame of mind and provide emotional support through expressed interest in what the person is experiencing. They also call upon the individual at least momentarily to consider a certain frame of mind even if to deny it. That may be enough for first approximations to begin.

If we are fairly certain about an individual's unexpressed frame of mind, we might become even more direct by *communicating what frame of mind we interpret to be primary.* Reverend Patel may say, "Fred, I suspect that you are feeling worse than you realize or are expressing." To the depressed person I could say, "You may be mulling over solutions more than you realize, or more than others ever expect." This approach asserts a particular frame of mind and tries to cut through an individual's denial or incognizance.

Finally, pastors might *communicate why the individual is misaligning his or her frame of mind.* At some point in her work, Reverend Patel may need to say, "What's happening, Fred, is that you're not talking about your feelings because you don't want to be upset." To the depressed man I might need to say, "You're acting as if everything is fine rather than expressing your private thoughts because you don't want to upset anyone with what's going on in your head." This approach explains why a certain frame of mind is not being communicated.

After each step of facilitation, we allow time for the individual to respond. If the person gives no indication of altering his or her form of communication to align with his or her silent frame of mind, we can then utilize another step further down the list. At each step pastors are not only naming the possible frame of mind of the individual, but also are subtly validating the appropriateness of that frame of mind and giving the individual permission to communicate it. Reverend Patel is conveying to Fred, "It's all right to talk about the feelings inside you," just as I am suggesting to the depressed person, "Telling about your plans, or coming fully to recognize your own plans, is extremely important."

In the examples for facilitating structure, the frame of mind content was broadly mentioned. Reverend Patel suggested to Fred that he might have feelings. I suggested to the man that he might be focusing on a plan or on solutions. In the process of aligning form and frame structure, such vague references are often sufficient. They can stimulate the individual to talk about content close to immediate lived experience so that form and frame content align.

That may not happen, however. As noted, people can align a form of communication structure with a corresponding frame of mind structure and yet not align form and frame content. I may gripe to my wife about certain things (my critical evaluative form of communication aligns with my critical evaluative frame of mind at the moment), but I may not gripe about what's really bothering me (central frame of mind content). Form and frame content remain misaligned. Sometimes this misalignment is intentional. I hold back central gripes until she takes responsibility for aligning my form and frame content by naming what is really bothering me. Other times I am truly not sure what my central gripes are (frame content) until I inadvertently hit upon them or someone articulates them for me.

When a content misalignment persists after a structural misalignment has been sufficiently rectified, we must then attend to this second-order communication problem. Based on what individuals have shared about their situation, plus our empathic imagining of their situation, we can try to help them match the content of their communication with the foreground content of their frame of mind. To do so we can use the same five approaches as when facilitating structure alignment. Once again, these approaches should merge naturally into the ongoing conversation with the individual.

Reverend Patel, for example, could begin by *communicating her own frame of mind content.* Fred may finally start to talk about feelings, but the feeling content may be about such things as fretting over having to miss a lot of work if Lois stays in the hospital. Acknowledging the content of her own feeling frame of mind, and hypothesizing that Fred may have similar content, she might say, "There are a lot of feelings about all this, but when you told me about Lois, the feeling that immediately came to me was fear that she would die." This intervention expresses her loving concern for Lois but also attempts to move Fred to communicate his own more pressing feelings.

In my other example, the depressed man eventually dropped his glibness and began to talk concretely about plans that had come to his mind since becoming despondent (a structural alignment was taking place). Those discussed plans, however, focused on such things as "reading lots of novels and going bowling with men from the church on Wednesdays." Acknowledging the content of my own pragmatic thoughts as I put myself in his depressed position, I said to him, "When I think about struggling with devastating situations, the weary thought sometimes comes to me that it would perhaps be easier to be dead than to go through the pain." This self-owned communication not only attempts to build a bridge of rapport with him, but to mobilize his own communication about such frame of mind content.

In a further effort to move Fred toward expression of central frame content, Reverend Patel could *communicate what frame content most people would probably have* in this circumstance: "When most people hear the word 'cancer,' they tend to worry about losing their loved one." Similarly, to facilitate expression of central content I might say to the depressed man, "It is not unusual for people to think about running away or dying as a way to escape from what seems like a hopeless situation."

Switching to a more personal approach, Reverend Patel could *ask about Fred's frame content:* "Have you been tied up in knots worrying about Lois dying?" Of the man I could ask, "Have you had any suicide thoughts or wishes?"

In an even more pointed attempt to help Fred communicate his frame of mind content, Reverend Patel could *communicate what frame content she interprets to be primary.* "Whether you recognize it or not, Fred, I think the possibility of losing Lois is deeply disturbing to you." I might say to the man, "I have a hunch that you've been thinking about killing yourself, or actually planning it."

Finally, we pastors may *communicate why the individual has misaligned frame of mind content.* Reverend Patel may say, "You're probably talking about feelings other than your feelings about Lois dying in part because it reminds you of the loss of your mother recently." To the depressed man I might say, "Maybe you're hesitant to express your suicide thoughts because you're afraid we'll stop you, even put you in the hospital."

In attempting to help individuals talk about what is really central to them (aligning form and frame content), I do not worry about suggesting wrong content. Even if I'm mistaken, my conjecture of what individuals might be thinking stimulates them to reflect on and express what is central in their frame of mind. Wrong content also motivates communication through individuals' natural inclination to correct others, especially when the errors are about themselves.

Neither do I worry about exact content. My effort is toward first approximations. If I can get individuals close to the central content of their frame of mind, that proximity tends to draw them toward the heart of the matter.

Finally, I am not overly concerned with infusing content, that is, the possibility of putting ideas in persons' minds so they communicate my frame of mind content as their own. In times of crisis, parishioners are often helped by borrowing my frame of mind content momentarily as they steady themselves to express their own. Unless an individual is chronically vulnerable, however, my suggested content will not influence him or her unless it has validity.

Facilitating intensity alignment is our next concern. The intensity of one's frame of mind tends to emerge as the person begins to communicate the central content of his or her frame of mind. This intensity can be expressed in a number of ways: vocal intensity, acted-out intensity, imaged intensity, and described intensity.

As Fred starts to focus more on the central content of his feeling frame of mind, he will likely begin to express it with the intensity affixed to it. His voice may reflect deep sadness or may vibrate with fear. He may get up and pace, wring his hands, or throw something. Conversely, he may stare, mumble, or remain inert. He may use strong words and vivid metaphors to convey the magnitude of his reaction. He may also express his intensity by describing his degree of preoccupation with a certain feeling or feeling state.

Alignment of intensity does not necessarily occur with the alignment of structure and content, however. Fred may stay businesslike even when talking about the possibility of losing Lois. Although the depressed man may communicate that he thinks about killing himself, he may not convey the seriousness of his thought. He may not give details of his thought (described intensity) or may not indicate with his tone of voice how resolute he is in killing himself (vocal intensity). To facilitate intensity alignment, pastors can use the same five approaches used to stimulate structure and content alignment.

We can *express our own frame of mind intensity* as a way of helping individuals express the intensity of their frame of mind. Realizing that the news about Lois moved her to tears, and empathetically imagining that Fred may have similar intensity of feeling, Reverend Patel might say in a genuinely tearful voice, "This news makes me want to cry, not just a little but a lot!" With descriptive intensity in mind, I might say to the depressed man, "A lot of pictures are coming to my mind when you tell me this: how you might do it, when you might do it, where you might do it, how you imagine people will react." The effort here is not so much to elicit information as to elicit energy, that is, the intensity attached to his suicide ideation.

In a further effort to facilitate expression, we might *communicate what frame intensity most people would probably have* in this circumstance. Using imaged intensity, Reverend Patel might say, "When people are first threatened with the loss of a loved one, they often feel a great wave of panic flood over them, like they did when they were a little boy or girl faced with something big and scary that they couldn't handle." She may also become dramatic with her voice as she accents key images like "great wave of panic" and "something big and scary" (vocalized intensity). She may put her hands up to her face like a little child who is trying to ward off something terrifying (acted-out intensity).

Using imaged intensity, I might say to the depressed man, "When some people think of killing themselves, they desperately hope that God's hand, or someone's hand, will come down to stop them. They desperately want to die, but they also desperately want to live." This statement may help clarify the man's ambivalent feelings about suicide, but its function here is to get him to express the intensity with which he holds life and death. More open communication about the intensity of his frame of mind may reduce his suicide impulse.

As a more direct approach, we can *ask an individual about the level of their intensity*. With described intensity in mind, Reverend Patel might say to Fred, "Are you finding yourself preoccupied with certain worries about Lois, or with certain ideas or feelings that keep coming back to you, even in your sleep?" To my despondent parishioner I might say, "Should I be worried about leaving you alone? Are you right on the verge of doing something to yourself if you find the right situation?"

Then again, we might *interpret what an individual's current intensity might be*. Using imaged and descriptive intensity, Reverend Patel might say, "You're tight as a drum, Fred. On a scale between zero and ten, with zero being not upset at all and ten being totally incapacitated, I think right now you're at a seven." "You're more dangerous to yourself than maybe you realize," I might say to the man. "There's a calm detachment as you talk about your plans which is ominous as hell."

Finally, and most directly, we can *communicate why there is misaligned intensity*. "Maybe you're talking in a low-key way that doesn't really fit with how intensely you feel about losing Lois, Fred, because you're afraid that if you let out even a little of the intensity, you'll be overwhelmed." "You may not share how intensely serious you are about killing yourself because you think that telling about it will take away from your motivation to do it."

Even if our attempts to elicit frame of mind intensity do not appear to work, we may still have been helpful. Individuals often vicariously experience the intensity others express for them, although in the long run that is not sufficient. Individuals will need to learn to express their own intensity of plan, feeling, thought, or judgment rather than live through others. But as a start, vicarious experience can be beneficial. Once again, we are aiming for first approximations.

In summary, dealing with communication misalignments requires these conceptual tools:

1. Four forms of communication
2. Four corresponding frames of mind
3. Three types of misalignment between form and frame: structure, content, and intensity

Overcoming misalignments begins with empathizing for alignment, which involves three steps:

1. Empathic listening
2. Empathic sensing
3. Empathic imagining

Facilitating alignment aims for first approximations—that is, helping the individual begin to communicate the structure, content, and intensity of his or her primary frame of mind. Toward that end we can use any of these five approaches:

1. Communicating our own frame of mind
2. Communicating the frame of mind of most people in a similar situation
3. Asking about a certain frame of mind
4. Interpreting a primary frame of mind
5. Explaining why a misalignment is happening

Applying this material on misalignment might at first seem too difficult. But it becomes easier as you realize that much of what I've said you've already been doing in some form or another. You'll also find your own way to utilize the suggestions I've made. The most important thing is to have a working approach, which the concepts of form of communication and corresponding frames of mind can supply.

We have been treating forms of communication as if they were tools we could alter for this purpose or that. They are, but they appear to be more. Forms of communication seem basic to who we are. They may be our primary ways of engaging the world. We tend to see the world through pragmatic eyes, feeling eyes, interpretative eyes, evaluative eyes. What meaning we give to our experiences, what structure we impose upon our life, we do through the framework of our basic ways of communicating.

Forms of communication are, in this sense, our fundamental perspectives on life. They are intrinsic to who we are and how we perceive life. Pastoral approaches to communication problems, consequently, deal with the very essence of our God-created existence. Let our communication work, therefore, be done skillfully, but with awe.

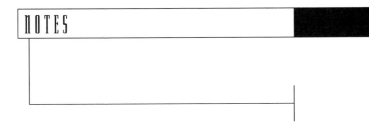

NOTES

1. BASIC FORMS OF COMMUNICATION

1. William James, *The Principles of Psychology* (1890; Cambridge: Harvard University Press, 1983), 273–78.

2. M. Scott Peck, *The Road Less Traveled* (New York: Simon & Schuster, 1978), 15.

3. James B. Nelson, *Embodiment: An Approach to Sexuality and Christian Theology* (Minneapolis: Augsburg Press, 1978), 31.

4. Charles V. Gerkin, *The Living Human Document: Re-Visioning Pastoral Counseling in a Hermeneutical Mode* (Nashville: Abingdon Press, 1984), 19–20.

5. Albert C. Outler, *Psychotherapy and the Christian Message* (New York: Harper & Row, 1954), 196.